4. 99

This book is to be returned on or before the last date stamped below or you will be charged a fine

New City College – Redbridge campus
Library and Learning Centre
Barley Lane
Romford RM6 4XT
https://towham.cirqahosting.com
Redbridge: 020 8548 7118

FARGO

Ethan Coen
and
Joel Coen

faber and faber

For Paul Gropman

First published in 1996
by Faber and Faber Limited
3 Queen Square London WC1N 3AU
This edition published in 2000

Photoset by Parker Typesetting Service, Leicester
Printed in Great Britain by
Mackays of Chatham PLC, Chatham, Kent

© Ethan Coen and Joel Coen, 1996
Photographs by James Bridges, Michael Tackett and Roger Deakins,
© Gramercy Pictures, 1996

Joel Coen and Ethan Coen are hereby identified as authors of this work in
accordance with Section 77 of the Copyright, Designs and Patents Act 1988

A CIP record for this book
is available from the British Library
ISBN 0-571-20244-6

2 4 6 8 10 9 7 5 3 1

CONTENTS

INTRODUCTION

Speaking of true stories, our grandmother told us this one. It happened in New York, many years ago.

Alone one day in her apartment, Grandma heard a knock at the door. She opened it to 'a large Negress', as she would later say, who, tired and thirsty, asked if she might have a glass of water. Grandma invited her to sit down in the foyer and went to get the water.

Grandma stopped before reaching the kitchen and returned to ask the woman if she wanted ice. She surprised the woman as she stood over a side table going through Grandma's handbag. As the Negress withdrew Grandma's wallet from the purse she looked up and, for a frozen moment, the two women stared at each other. Then Grandma leapt.

She grabbed the arm that held the wallet. A struggle. The Negress reared back and swung her free hand at Grandma's face. Grandma's glasses flew off, hit the floor and shattered, but Grandma hung on tenaciously. Grandma dug her fingernails into the Negress's wrist. The Negress howled, dropped the wallet and fled.

Grandma told the story of the large Negress many times and we never tired of it – the innocent ringing of the doorbell, the meeting, the startling character reversal, then the drama of the slapfight. Grandma always became agitated at the point where the Negress hits her and her glasses fly off; the digging of the fingernails into the wrist is always presented as a great brainwave, and the howl of the predatory Negress being put to flight is not just the story's climax, but a shocking culmination of the woman's metamorphosis from meek water-seeker to raging harpy.

Either by virtue of its drama or its repetition, the story came to feel mythic. One pictures the black woman a huge Southern Baptist with a sun hat, reading glasses and mountainous bosoms. Grandma, a small wiry Russian, is flying at her like a dog at a rearing bear. The eyes of the black woman roll with fear and rage. Her floral print dress is frozen mid-swirl with the twist of her body; one hand, flung back, clutches the wallet towards which Grandma, teeth bared in a snarl, leaps. 'Grandma and the Negress' – it is a theme that might have inspired great artists through the ages.

But in retrospect some elements of Grandma's story test credulity. Do eyeglasses really 'shatter' when they hit the floor? Do people who are tired and thirsty really ascend to twelfth-floor apartments on West End Avenue seeking glasses of water? If not, would a burglar use such a story? And even if so, would it work, even on Grandma? And then – how exactly did the fat woman flee? Did she stampede, wheezing, bosoms a-jostle, down twelve flights of stairs? Or did she summon the elevator and anxiously wait, hopping from foot to foot, humming old temperance songs?

One is forced to wonder about the other 'true' stories that Grandma told us. Having grown up in Tsaritsin (later renamed Stalingrad and, later still, Volgograd), did she really almost drown on a flatboat on the Volga River? Well, why not? But did her cousin, who became an officer in the Red Army, really marry a beautiful woman who from her wedding night on did not rise from bed where she passed the time eating chocolates and waxing fatter and fatter until (and perhaps past) the day when her husband – appalled, frustrated, despondent – shot himself?

Grandma said so. They are true stories; they happened like this. You might think that by virtue of their setting alone they would be incredible to two children growing up in suburban Minneapolis. But no, we accepted all of her stories, either because children are credulous, or because *we* were credulous, or because the frozen plains of Minnesota are not so different from those outside Tsaritsin. And then, also, our grandmother was not unique even in our Midwestern town. Mar Ralnick, a teacher in our Hebrew school, would tell us about how when he was a youth the Cossacks would break into his family's house – in his account it sounded like a daily occurrence – searching for sacks of grain. Young Mar Ralnick would tell the Cossacks that there was no grain. One day he did so with too little respect, and one of the Cossacks took umbrage. 'And then,' said Mar Ralnick, now an elderly man with Hubblesque eyeglasses, vein-roped hands and waggling jowels, 'the Cossack let me feel his whip.' The tension between the familiar (Mar Ralnick) and the exotic (whip-wielding Cossack) is striking only now, years later, in retrospect. At the time it did not seem strange that these Cossacks searching for sacks of grain should tramp so close to one's own experience. But even if it is strange, *that* is no evidence that the thing didn't happen – just as the relative banality of Grandma's adventure with the Negress is no guarantee of its truth.

It is a fact, speaking of Russia, true stories and personal perspective, that Leon Trotsky lived briefly on Vyse Avenue in the Bronx; a headline in a local paper in October of 1917 read: 'Bronx Man Leads Russian Revolution.'

Why not believe it? The world, however wide, has folds and wrinkles that bring distant places together in strange ways. An adage says: 'All politics is local.' This is a special case of the truism that all experience is personal. A corollary is that in some sense there is no exotica. Everything gets compared to your own experience. Paradoxically, what is closest to home can seem exotic. We can't read about the South Seas without comparing it to Minneapolis, and can't describe Minneapolis, even to ourselves, without it seeming like the South Seas.

But to return to Grandma. She emigrated from Tsaritsin to New York as an adolescent after the Revolution. About seventy-five years later she began to lose her memory. It went quickly; her speech lost its sense and then she stopped speaking English altogether. For the last year of her life she did speak – Russian. She hadn't used her mother tongue in almost eighty years, or had used it rarely – for some reason she encouraged us to memorize the phrase 'Yayik do Kieva Dovedet', meaning 'By your tongue you will get to Kiev', a maxim whose sense is, 'If you don't know, just ask'. What use she thought we might find for that phrase in Minneapolis, we don't know. But picture the world as Grandma might have, as a great ball thinly crusted with oceans, soil and snow. People crawl across this thin crust to arrive at some improbable place where they meet other crawling people. Some of these people are Red Russians, some of these people are White Russians, some of these people are not Russians at all. They do various improbable things with and to each other, and later tell stories about the things they did, stories having greater and lesser fidelity to truth. The stories that are not credible will occasionally, however, turn out to be true, and stories that *are* credible will conversely turn out to be false. Surely young Grandma (itself a paradox) would not have believed anyone telling her that she would never in her life see Kiev, but *would* see The Jolly Troll Smorgasbord & Family Restaurant in Minneapolis.

The story that follows is about Minnesota. It evokes the abstract landscape of our childhood – a bleak, windswept tundra, resembling Siberia except for its Ford dealerships and Hardee's restaurants. It aims to be both homey and exotic, and pretends to be true.

Ethan Coen
1996

The following text fades in over black:

This is a true story. The events depicted in this film took place in Minnesota in 1987. At the request of the survivors, the names have been changed. Out of respect for the dead, the rest has been told exactly as it occurred.

FLARE TO WHITE

FADE IN FROM WHITE

Slowly the white becomes a barely perceptible image: white particles wave over a white background. A snowfall.

A car bursts through the curtain of snow.

The car is equipped with a hitch and is towing another car, a brand-new light brown Cutlass Ciera with the pink sales sticker showing in its rear window.

As the cars roar past, leaving snow swirling in their draft, the title of the film fades in.

FARGO

Green highway signs point the way to MOOREHEAD, MINNESOTA/ FARGO, NORTH DAKOTA. *The roads for the two cities diverge. A sign says* WELCOME TO NORTH DAKOTA *and another just after says* NOW ENTERING FARGO, ND, POP. 44,412.

The car pulls into a Rodeway Inn.

HOTEL LOBBY

A man in his early forties, balding and starting to paunch, goes to the reception desk. The clerk is an older woman.

CLERK

And how are you today, sir?

MAN

Real good now. I'm checking in – Mr Anderson.

The man prints 'Jerry Lundega–' onto a registration card, then hastily crosses out the last name and starts to print 'Anderson'.

As she types into a computer:

CLERK

Okay, Mr Anderson, and you're still planning on staying with us just the one night, then?

ANDERSON

You bet.

HOTEL ROOM

The man turns on the TV, which shows the local evening news.

NEWS ANCHOR

– whether they will go to summer camp at all. Katie Jensen has more.

KATIE

It was supposed to be a project funded by the city council; it was supposed to benefit those Fargo–Moorehead children who would otherwise not be able to afford a lakeshore summer camp. But nobody consulted city comptroller Stu Jacobson . . .

CHAIN RESTAURANT

Anderson sits alone at a table finishing dinner. Muzak plays. A middle-aged waitress approaches holding a pot of regular coffee in one hand and decaf in the other.

WAITRESS

Can I warm that up for ya there?

ANDERSON

You bet.

The man looks at his watch.

THROUGH A WINDSHIELD

*We are pulling into the snowswept parking lot of a one-story brick
building. Broken neon at the top of the building identifies it as the Jolly
Troll Tavern. A troll, also in neon, holds a champagne glass aloft.*

INSIDE

*The bar is downscale even for this town. Country music plays on the
jukebox.*

*Two men are seated in a booth at the back. One is short, slight,
youngish. The other man is somewhat older, and dour. The table in
front of them is littered with empty long-neck beer bottles. The ashtray is
full.*

Anderson approaches.

ANDERSON

I'm, uh, Jerry Lundegaard –

YOUNGER MAN

You're Jerry Lundegaard?

JERRY

Yah, Shep Proudfoot said –

YOUNGER MAN

Shep said you'd be here at 7.30. What gives, man?

JERRY

Shep said 8.30.

YOUNGER MAN

We been sitting here an hour. I've peed three times already.

JERRY

I'm sure sorry. I – Shep told me 8.30. It was a mix-up, I guess.

YOUNGER MAN

Ya got the car?

JERRY

Yah, you bet. It's in the lot there. Brand-new burnt umber Ciera.

3

Yeah, okay. Well, siddown, then. I'm Carl Showalter and this is my associate Gaear Grimsrud.

JERRY

Yah, how ya doin'. So, uh, we all set on this thing, then?

CARL

Sure, Jerry, we're all set. Why wouldn't we be?

JERRY

Yah, no, I'm sure you are. Shep vouched for you and all. I got every confidence here in you fellas.

They stare at him. An awkward beat.

. . . So I guess that's it, then. Here's the keys –

CARL

No, that's not it, Jerry.

JERRY

. . . Huh?

CARL

The new vehicle, plus forty thousand dollars.

JERRY

Yah, but the deal was, the car first, see, then the forty thousand, like as if it was the ransom. I thought Shep told you –

CARL

Shep didn't tell us much, Jerry.

JERRY

Well, okay, it's –

CARL

Except that you were gonna be here at 7.30.

JERRY

Yah, well, that was a mix-up, then.

CARL

Yeah, you already said that.

JERRY

Yah. But it's not a whole pay-in-advance deal. I give you a brand-new vehicle in advance and –

CARL

I'm not gonna debate you, Jerry.

JERRY

Okay.

CARL

I'm not gonna sit here and debate. I will say this, though: what Shep told us didn't make a whole lot of sense.

JERRY

Oh, no, it's real sound. It's all worked out.

CARL

You want your own wife kidnapped?

JERRY

Yah.

Carl stares. Jerry looks blankly back.

CARL

. . . You – my point is, you pay the ransom – what, eighty thousand bucks? – I mean, you give us half the ransom, forty thousand, you keep half. It's like robbing Peter to pay Paul, it doesn't make any –

JERRY

Okay, it's – see, it's not me payin' the ransom. The thing is, my wife, she's wealthy – her dad, he's real well off. Now, I'm in a bit of trouble –

CARL

What kind of trouble are you in, Jerry?

JERRY

Well, that's, that's, I'm not gonna go inta, inta – see, I just need money. Now, her dad's real wealthy –

CARL

So why don't you just ask him for the money?

Grimsrud, the dour man who has not yet spoken, now softly puts in with a Swedish-accented voice:

GRIMSRUD

Or your fucking wife, you know.

CARL

Or your fucking wife, Jerry.

JERRY

Well, it's all just part of this – they don't know I need it, see. Okay, so there's that. And even if they did, I wouldn't get it. So there's that on top, then. See, these're personal matters.

CARL

Personal matters.

JERRY

Yah. Personal matters that needn't, uh –

CARL

Okay, Jerry. You're tasking us to perform this mission, but you, you won't, uh, you won't – aw, fuck it, let's take a look at that Ciera.

MINNEAPOLIS SUBURBAN HOUSE

Jerry enters through the kitchen door, in a parka and a red plaid Elmer Fudd hat. He stamps snow off his feet. He is carrying a bag of groceries which he deposits on the kitchen counter.

JERRY

Hon? Got the growshries.

VOICE

Thank you, hon. How's Fargo?

JERRY

Yah, real good.

VOICE

Dad's here.

DEN

Jerry enters, pulling off his plaid cap.

JERRY

How ya doin', Wade?

Wade Gustafson is mid-sixtyish, vigorous, with a full head of gray hair. His eyes remain fixed on the TV.

WADE

Yah, pretty good.

JERRY

Whatcha watchin' there?

WADE

Norstars.

JERRY

. . . Who they playin'?

WADE

OOOoooh!

His reaction synchronizes with a reaction from the crowd.

KITCHEN

Jerry walks back in, taking off his coat. His wife is putting on an apron. Jerry nods toward the living room.

JERRY

Is he stayin' for supper, then?

WIFE

Yah, I think so . . . Dad, are you stayin' for supper?

WADE
(*off*)

Yah.

DINING ROOM

Jerry, his wife, Wade and Scotty, twelve years old, sit eating.

SCOTTY

May I be excused?

JERRY

Sure, ya done there?

SCOTTY

Uh-huh. Goin' out.

WIFE

Where are you going?

SCOTTY

Just out. Just McDonald's.

JERRY

Back at 9.30.

SCOTTY

Okay.

WADE

He just ate. And he didn't finish. He's going to McDonald's instead of finishing here?

WIFE

He sees his friends there. It's okay.

WADE

It's okay? McDonald's? What do you think they do there? They don't drink milkshakes, I assure you!

WIFE

It's okay, Dad.

JERRY

Wade, have ya had a chance to think about, uh, that deal I was talkin' about, those forty acres there on Wayzata.

WADE

You told me about it.

JERRY

Yah, you said you'd have a think about it. I understand it's a lot of money –

WADE

A heck of a lot. What'd you say you were gonna put there?

JERRY

A lot. It's a limited –

WADE

I know it's a lot.

JERRY

I mean a parking lot.

WADE

Yah, well, seven hundred and fifty thousand dollars is a lot – ha ha ha!

JERRY

Yah, well, it's a chunk, but –

WADE

I had a couple lots, late fifties. Lost a lot of money. A 'lot' of money.

JERRY

Yah, but –

WADE

I thought you were gonna show it to Stan Grossman. He passes on this stuff before it gets kicked up to me.

JERRY

Well, you know Stan'll say no dice. That's why you pay him. I'm asking *you* here, Wade. This could work out real good for me and Jean and Scotty –

WADE

Jean and Scotty never have to worry.

WHITE

A black line curls through the white. Twisting perspective shows that it is an aerial shot of a two-lane highway, bordered by snowfields. The highway carries one moving car.

INT. CAR

Carl Showalter is driving. Gaear Grimsrud stares blankly out.

After a long beat:

GRIMSRUD

Where is Pancakes Hause?

CARL

What?

GRIMSRUD

We stop at Pancakes Hause.

CARL

What're you, nuts? We had pancakes for breakfast. I gotta go somewhere I can get a shot and a beer – and a steak maybe. Not more fuckin' pancakes. Come on.

Grimsrud gives him a sour look.

. . . Come on, man. Okay, here's an idea. We'll stop outside of Brainerd. I know a place there we can get laid. Wuddya think?

GRIMSRUD

I'm fucking hungry now, you know.

CARL

Yeah, yeah, Jesus – I'm sayin', we'll stop for pancakes, then we'll get laid. Wuddya think?

GUSTAFSON OLDS GARAGE

Jerry is sitting in his glassed-in salesman's cubicle just off the showroom floor. On the other side of his desk sit an irate customer and his wife.

CUSTOMER

We sat here right in this room and went over this and over this!

JERRY

Yah, but that TruCoat –

CUSTOMER

I sat right here and said I didn't want no TruCoat!

JERRY

Yah, but I'm sayin', that TruCoat, you don't get it and you get oxidization problems. It'll cost you a heck of a lot more'n five hunnert –

CUSTOMER

You're sittin' here, you're talkin' in circles! You're talkin' like we didn't go over this already!

JERRY

Yah, but this TruCoat –

CUSTOMER

We had us a deal here for nineteen-five. You sat there and darned if you didn't tell me you'd get me this car, these options, WITHOUT THE SEALANT, for nineteen-five!

JERRY

Okay, I'm not sayin' I didn't –

CUSTOMER

You called me twenty minutes ago and said you had it! Ready to make delivery, ya says! Come on down and get it! And here ya are and you're wastin' *my* time and you're wastin' my *wife's* time and I'm payin' nineteen-five for this vehicle here!

JERRY

Well, okay, I'll talk to my boss . . .

He rises and, as he leaves:

. . . See, they install that TruCoat at the factory, there's nothin' we can do, but I'll talk to my boss.

The couple watch him go to a nearby cubicle.

CUSTOMER

These guys here – these guys! It's always the same! It's always more! He's a liar!

WIFE

Please, dear.

CUSTOMER

We went over this and over this –

Jerry sits perched on the desk of another salesman who is eating lunch as he watches a hockey game on a small portable TV.

JERRY

So you're goin' to the Gophers on Sunday?

SALESMAN

You bet.

JERRY

You wouldn't have an extra ticket there?

SALESMAN

They're playin' the Buckeyes!

JERRY

Yah.

SALESMAN

You kiddin'!

JERRY'S CUBICLE

Jerry re-enters.

JERRY

Well, he never done this before, but seein' as it's special circumstances and all, he says I can knock one hunnert off that TruCoat.

CUSTOMER

One hundred! You lied to me, Mr Lundegaard. You're a bald-faced liar!

Jerry sits staring at his lap.

. . . A fucking liar –

WIFE

Bucky, please!

Jerry mumbles into his lap:

One hunnert's the best we can do here.

CUSTOMER

Oh, for Christ sake, where's my goddamn checkbook. Let's get this over with.

WIDE EXTERIOR: TRUCK STOP

There is a restaurant with many big rigs parked nearby, and a motel with an outsize Paul Bunyan and Babe the Blue Ox flanking its sign: BLUE OX MOTEL.

MOTEL ROOM

Carl Showalter and Gaear Grimsrud are in the twin beds having sex with two truck-stop hookers.

CARL

Oh, Jesus, yeah.

HIS HOOKER

There ya go, sugar.

GRIMSRUD

Nnph.

HIS HOOKER

Yeah. Yeah. Oh, yeah.

LATER

The couples lie in their respective beds, gazing at the offscreen TV.

ED MCMAHON

– Johnny's guests tonight will be Lee Majors, George Wendt and Steve Boutsikaros from the San Diego Zoo, so keep that dial –

LUNDEGAARD KITCHEN

We hear a morning show on the television. Jean Lundegaard is making coffee in the kitchen as Scott eats cereal at the table.

                              JEAN
I'm talkin' about your potential.

                              SCOTT
                            (*absently*)
Uh-huh.

                              JEAN
You're not a C student.

                              SCOTT
Uhn.

                              JEAN
And yet you're gettin' C grades. It's this disparity there that
concerns your dad and me.

                              SCOTT
Uh-huh.

                              JEAN
You know what a disparity is?

                              SCOTT
                            (*testily*)
Yeah!

                              JEAN
Okay. Well, that's why we don't want ya goin' out fer hockey.

                              SCOTT
Oh, man!

    The phone rings.

. . . What's the big deal? It's an hour –

                              JEAN
Hold on.

    She picks up the phone.

. . . Hello?

                           PHONE VOICE
Yah, hiya, hon.

Oh, hiya, Dad.

Jerry around?

JEAN

Yah, he's still here – I'll catch him for ya.

She holds the phone away and calls:

. . . Hon?

VOICE

Yah.

JEAN

It's Dad.

VOICE

Yah . . .

Jerry enters in shirtsleeves and tie.

. . . Yah, okay . . .

SCOTT

Look, Dad, there is no fucking way –

JEAN

Scott!

JERRY

Say, let's watch the language –

He takes the phone.

. . . How ya doin', Wade?

WADE

What's goin' on there?

JERRY

Oh, nothing, Wade. How ya doin' there?

WADE

Stan Grossman looked at your proposal. Says it's pretty sweet.

17

JERRY

No kiddin'?

WADE

We might be innarested.

JERRY

No kiddin'! I'd need the cash pretty quick there. In order to close the deal.

WADE

Come by at 2.30 and we'll talk about it. If your numbers are right, Stan says its pretty sweet. Stan Grossman.

JERRY

Yah.

WADE

2.30.

Click. Dial tone.

JERRY

Yah, okay.

GUSTAFSON OLDS GARAGE

Jerry wanders through the service area where cars are being worked on. He stops by an Indian in blue jeans who is looking at the underside of a car that sits on a hydraulic lift with a cage light hanging off its innards.

JERRY

Say, Shep, how ya doin' there?

SHEP

Mm.

JERRY

Say, ya know those two fellas ya put me in touch with, up there in Fargo?

SHEP

Put you in touch with Grimsrud.

JERRY

Well, yah, but he had a buddy there. He, uh –

SHEP

Well, I don't vouch for him.

JERRY

Well, that's okay, I just –

SHEP

I vouch for Grimsrud. Who's his buddy?

JERRY

Carl somethin'?

SHEP

Never heard of him. Don't vouch for him.

JERRY

Well, that's okay, he's a buddy of the guy ya vouched for, so I'm not worryin'. I just, I was wonderin', see, I gotta get in touch with 'em – see, this deal I needed 'em for, I might not need it anymore, sumpn's happenin', see –

SHEP

Call'm up.

JERRY

Yah, well, see, I did that, and I haven't been able to get 'em, so I thought you maybe'd know an alternate number or what have ya.

SHEP

Nope.

Jerry slaps his fist into his open palm and snaps his fingers.

JERRY

Okay, well, real good, then.

CAR

Carl is driving. Grimsrud stares out the front.

After a beat:

CARL

. . . Look at that. Twin Cities. IDS Building, the big glass one.
Tallest skyscraper in the Midwest. After the Sears, uh, Chicago
. . . You never been to Minneapolis?

GRIMSRUD

No.

CARL

. . . Would it kill you to say something?

GRIMSRUD

I did.

CARL

'No.' First thing you've said in the last four hours. That's a, that's
a fountain of conversation, man. That's a geyser. I mean, whoa,
daddy, stand back, man. Shit, I'm sittin' here driving, man, doin'
all the driving, whole fucking way from Brainerd, drivin', tryin' to,
you know, tryin' to chat, keep our spirits up, fight the boredom of
the road, and you can't say one fucking thing just in the way of
conversation.

Grimsrud smokes, gazing out the window.

. . . Well, fuck it, I don't have to talk either, man. See how *you* like
it.

Carl looks at Grimsrud for a reaction.

. . . Just total fuckin' silence. Two can play at *that* game, smart
guy. We'll just see how *you* like it . . .

He drives.

. . . Total silence . . .

JERRY'S CUBICLE

He is on the phone.

JERRY

Yah, real good. How you doin'?

VOICE

Pretty good, Mr Lundegaard. You're damned hard to get on the phone.

JERRY

Yah, it's pretty darned busy here, but that's the way we like it.

VOICE

That's for sure. Now, I just need, on these last, these financing documents you sent us, I can't read the serial numbers of the vehicles on here, so I –

JERRY

But I already got the, it's okay, the loans are in place, I already got the, the what, the –

VOICE

Yeah, the three hundred and twenty thousand dollars, you got the money last month.

JERRY

Yah, so we're all set.

VOICE

Yeah, but the vehicles you were borrowing on, I just can't read the serial numbers on your application. Maybe if you could just read them to me –

JERRY

But the deal's already done, I already got the money –

VOICE

Yeah, but we have an audit here, I just have to know that these vehicles you're financing with this money, that they really exist.

JERRY

Yah, well, they exist all right.

VOICE

I'm sure they do – ha ha! But I can't read their serial numbers here. So if you could read me –

JERRY

Well, but see, I don't have 'em in front a me – why don't I just fax you over a copy –

No, fax is no good, that's what I have and I can't read the darn
thing –

JERRY

Yah, okay, I'll have my girl send you a copy, then.

VOICE

Okay, because if I can't correlate this note with the specific
vehicles, then I gotta call back that money –

JERRY

Yah, how much money was that?

VOICE

Three hundred and twenty thousand dollars. See, I gotta correlate
that money with the cars it's being lent on.

JERRY

Yah, no problem, I'll just fax that over to ya, then.

VOICE

No, no, fax is –

JERRY

I mean send it over. I'll shoot it right over to ya.

VOICE

Okay.

JERRY

Okay, real good, then.

CLOSE ON TELEVISION

*A morning-show host in an apron stands behind a counter on a kitchen
set.*

HOST

So I separate the – how the heck do I get the egg out of the shell
without breaking it?

*Jean Lundegaard is curled up on the couch with a cup of coffee,
watching the television.*

HOSTESS

You just prick a little hole in the end and blow!

Jean smiles as we hear laughter and applause from the studio audience. She hears something else – a faint scraping sound – and looks up.

HOST

Okay, here goes nothing.

The scraping sound persists. Jean sets down her coffee cup and rises.

From the studio audience:

AUDIENCE

Awoooo!

KITCHEN

We track toward the back door. A curtain is stretched tight across its window.

Jean pulls the curtain back. Bright sunlight amplified by snow floods in.

A man in an orange ski mask looks up from the lock.

Jean gasps, drops the curtain, turns and runs into –

– a taller man, also in a ski mask, already in the house.

We hear the crack of the back-door window being smashed.

The tall man – Gaear Grimsrud – grabs Jean's wrist.

She screams, staring at her own imprisoned wrist, then wraps her gaping mouth around Grimsrud's gloved thumb and bites down hard.

He drops her wrist. As Carl enters, she races up the stairs.

GRIMSRUD

Unguent.

CARL

Huh?

Grimsrud looks at his thumb.

GRIMSRUD

I need . . . unguent.

UPSTAIRS BEDROOM

As the two men enter, a door at the far side is slamming shut. A cord snakes in under the door.

MASTER BATHROOM

Jean, sobbing, frantically pushes at buttons on the princess phone.

The phone pops out of her hands, jangles across the tile floor, smashes against the door and then bounces away, its cord ripped free.

With a groaning sound, the door shifts in its frame.

BEDROOM

Grimsrud has a crowbar jammed in between the bathroom door and frame, and is working it.

BATHROOM

Jean crosses to a high window above the toilet and throws it open. Snow

24

that had drifted against the window sifts lightly in. Jean steps up onto the toilet.

The door creaks, moving as one piece in its frame.

Jean glances back as she steps up from the toilet seat to the tank.

The groaning of the door ends with the wood around its knob splintering and the knob itself falling out onto the floor.

The door swings open.

Grimsrud and Carl enter.

THEIR POV

Room empty, window open.

Carl strides to the window and hoists himself out.

Grimsrud opens the medicine cabinet and delicately taps aside various bottles and tubes, seeking the proper unguent.

He finds a salve but after a moment sets it down, noticing something in the mirror.

The shower curtain is drawn around the tub.

He steps toward it.

As he reaches for the curtain, it explodes outward, animated by thrashing limbs.

Jean, screaming, tangled in the curtain, rips it off its rings and stumbles out into the bedroom. Grimsrud follows.

BEDROOM

Jean rushes toward the door, cloaked by the shower curtain but awkwardly trying to push it off.

UPSTAIRS LANDING

Still thrashing, Jean crashes against the upstairs railing, trips on the curtain and falls, thumping crazily down the stairs.

Grimsrud trots down after her.

INT. WADE'S OFFICE

Wade sits behind his desk; another man rises as Jerry enters.

                    JERRY
How ya doin' there, Stan? How are ya, Wade?

   Stan Grossman shakes his hand.

                    STAN
Good to see ya again, Jerry. If these numbers are right, this looks
pretty sweet.

                    JERRY
Oh, those numbers are right all right, bleemee.

                    WADE
This is do-able.

                    STAN
Congratulations, Jerry.

                    JERRY
Yah, thanks, Stan, it's a pretty –

                    WADE
What kind of finder's fee were you looking for?

                    JERRY
. . . Huh?

                    STAN
The financials are pretty thorough, so the only thing we don't
know is your fee.

                    JERRY
. . . My fee? Wade, what the heck're you talkin' about?

                    WADE
Stan and I're okay.

26

JERRY

Yah.

WADE

We're good to load in.

JERRY

Yah.

WADE

But we never talked about your fee for bringin' it to us.

JERRY

No, but, Wade, see, I was bringin' you this deal for you to loan *me* the money to put in. It's my deal here, see?

Wade scowls, looks at Stan.

STAN

Jerry – we thought you were bringin' us an investment.

JERRY

Yah, right –

STAN

You're sayin' – what're you sayin'?

WADE

You're sayin' that we put in all the money and you collect when it pays off?

JERRY

No, no. I – I'd, I'd – pay you back the principal, and interest – heck, I'd go – one over prime –

STAN

We're not a bank, Jerry.

Wade is angry.

WADE

What the heck, Jerry, if I wanted *bank* interest on seven hunnert'n fifty thousand I'd go to Midwest Federal. Talk to Bill Diehl.

STAN

He's at Norstar.

WADE

He's at –

JERRY

No, see, I don't need a finder's fee, I need – finder's fee's, what, ten percent, heck that's not gonna do it for me. I need the principal.

STAN

Jerry, we're not going to just *give* you seven hundred and fifty thousand dollars.

WADE

What the heck were you thinkin'? Heck, if I'm only gettin' bank interest, I'd look for complete security. Heck, FDIC. I don't see nothin' like *that* here.

JERRY

Yah, but I – okay, I would, I'd guarantee ya your money back.

WADE

I'm not talkin' about your damn *word*, Jerry. Geez, what the heck're you? . . . Well, look, I don't want to cut you out of the loop, but this here's a good deal. I assume, if you're not innarested, you won't mind if we move on it innapendently.

28

PARKING LOT

We are high and wide on the office building's parking lot. Jerry emerges wrapped in a parka, his arms sticking stiffly out at his sides, his breath vaporizing. He goes to his car, opens its front door, pulls out a red plastic scraper and starts methodically scraping off the thin crust of ice that has developed on his windshield.

The scrape-scrape-scrape sound carries in the frigid air.

Jerry goes into a frenzy, banging the scraper against the windshield and the hood of his car.

The tantrum passes. Jerry stands panting, staring at nothing in particular.

Scrape-scrape-scrape – he goes back to work on the windshield.

FRONT DOOR

A beat, silent but for a key scraping at the lock.

The door swings open and Jerry edges in, looking about, holding a sack of groceries.

                                          JERRY
Hon?

   He shuts the door.

. . . Got the growshries . . .

   He has already seen the shower curtain on the floor. He frowns, pokes at it with his foot.

. . . Hon?

UPSTAIRS BATHROOM

Jerry walks in. He sets the groceries down on the toilet tank.

He looks at the open window, through which snow still sifts in. He shuts it.

He picks up the small tube of unguent that sits on the sink, frowns at it, puts it back in the medicine chest.

He looks at the shower curtain rod holding empty rings.

FOYER

Once again we are looking at the rumpled shower curtain.

From another room:

JERRY'S VOICE

Yah, Wade, I – it's Jerry, I.

   Then, slightly more agitated:

. . . Yah, Wade, it's, I, it's Jerry . . .

   Beat.

. . . Wade, it's Jerry, I – we gotta talk, Wade, it's terrible . . .

   Beat.

LIVING ROOM

Jerry stands in wide shot, hands on hips, looking down at a telephone.

After a motionless beat he picks up the phone and punches in a number.

. . . Yah, Wade Gustafson, please.

BLACK

Hold in black.

A slow tilt down from night sky brings the head of a large papier-mâché figure into frame. It is a flannel-shirted woodsman carrying a double-edged ax over one shoulder. As we hear the rumble of an approaching car, the continuing tilt and boom down brings us down the woodsman's body to a pedestal.

A sweep of headlights illuminates a sign on the pedestal: WELCOME TO BRAINERD – HOME OF PAUL BUNYAN.

The headlights sweep off and a car hums past and on into the background. The two-lane highway is otherwise empty.

INT. CAR

Carl drives. Grimsrud smokes and gazes out the window. From the back seat we hear whimpering.

Grimsrud twists to look.

Jean lies bound and curled on the back seat underneath a tarpaulin.

GRIMSRUD
Shut the fuck up or I'll throw you back in the trunk, you know.

CARL
Geez. That's more'n I've heard you say all week.

Grimsrud stares at him, then turns back to the window.

At a loud WHOOP Carl starts and looks back out the rear window. Fifty yards behind a state trooper has turned on his gumballs.

Carl eases the car onto the shoulder.

CARL
Ah, shit, the tags . . .

Grimsrud looks at him.

. . . It's just the tags. I never put my tags on the car. Don't worry, I'll take care of this.

He looks into the back seat as the car bounces and slows on the gravel shoulder.

. . . Let's keep still back there, lady, or we're gonna have to, ya know, to shoot ya.

Grimsrud stares at Carl.

. . . Hey! I'll take care of this!

Both cars have stopped. Carl looks up at the rear-view mirror.

The trooper is stopped on the shoulder just behind them, writing in his citation book.

Carl watches.

We hear the trooper's door open.

The trooper walks up the shoulder, one hand resting lightly on top of his holster, his breath steaming in the cold night air.

Carl opens his window as the trooper draws up.

How can I help you, officer?

The trooper scans the inside of the car, taking his time.

Grimsrud smokes and gazes calmly out his window.

Finally:

TROOPER

This a new car, then, sir?

CARL

It certainly is, officer. Still got that smell!

TROOPER

You're required to display temporary tags, either in the plate area or taped inside the back window.

CARL

Certainly –

TROOPER

Can I see your license and registration please?

CARL

Certainly.

He reaches for his wallet.

. . . I was gonna tape up the temporary tag, ya know, to be in full compliance, but it, uh, it, uh . . . must a slipped my mind . . .

He extends his wallet toward the trooper, a folded fifty-dollar bill protruding from it.

. . . So maybe the best thing would be to take care of that, right here in Brainerd.

TROOPER

What's this sir?

CARL

That's my license and registration. I wanna be in compliance.

He forces a laugh.

. . . I was just thinking I could take care of it right here. In Brainerd.

The policeman thoughtfully pats the fifty into the billfold and hands the billfold back into the car.

TROOPER

Put that back in your pocket, please.

Carl's nervous smile fades.

. . . And step out of the car please, sir.

Grimsrud, smiling thinly, shakes his head.

There is a whimpering sound.

The policeman hesitates.

Another sound.

The policeman leans forward into the car, listening.

Grimsrud reaches across Carl, grabs the trooper by the hair and slams his head down onto the car door.

The policeman grunts, digs awkwardly for footing outside and throws an arm for balance against the outside of the car.

With his free hand, Grimsrud pops the glove compartment. He brings a gun out and reaches across Carl and shoots – BANG – into the back of the trooper's head.

Jean screams.

GRIMSRUD

Shut up.

He releases the policeman.

The policeman's head slides out the window and his body flops back onto the street.

Carl looks out at the cop in the road.

CARL
(*softly*)

Whoa . . . Whoa, Daddy.

Grimsrud takes the trooper's hat off of Carl's lap and sails it out the open window.

GRIMSRUD

You'll take care of it. Boy, you are smooth smooth, you know.

CARL

Whoa, Daddy.

Jean, for some reason, screams again. Then stops.

GRIMSRUD

Clear him off the road.

CARL

Yeah.

He gets out.

EXT. ROAD

Carl leans down to hoist up the body.

Headlights appear: an oncoming car.

INT. CIERA

Grimsrud notices.

EXT. ROAD

The car approaches, slowing.

Carl, with the trooper's body hoisted halfway up, is frozen in the headlights.

The car accelerates and roars past and away. We just make out the silhouettes of two occupants in front.

INT. CIERA

Grimsrud slides into the driver's seat. He squeals into a U-turn, the driver's door slamming shut with his spin.

Small red tail lights fishtail up ahead. The pursued car churns up fine snow.

Grimsrud takes the cigarette from his mouth and stubs it in his ashtray. We hear the churning of the car wheels and the pinging of snow clods and salt on the car's underside.

In the back seat, Jean starts screaming.

Grimsrud is not gaining on the tail lights.

He fights with the wheel as his car swims on the road face.

The red tail lights ahead start to turn. With a distant crunching sound, they disappear.

The headlights now show only empty road, starting to turn.

Grimsrud frowns and slows.

His headlights show the car up ahead off the road, crumpled around a telephone pole, having failed to hold a turn.

Grimsrud brakes.

Jean slides off the back seat and thumps into the legwell.

Grimsrud sweeps his gun off the front seat, throws open his door and gets out.

EXT. ROAD

The wrecked car's headlights shine off into a snowfield abutting the highway. A young man in a down parka is limping across the snowfield, away from his wrecked car.

Grimsrud strides calmly out after the injured boy. He raises his gun and fires.

With a poof of feathers, a hole opens up in the boy's back and he pitches into the snow.

Grimsrud walks up to the wreck and peers in its half-open door.

A young woman is trapped inside the twisted wreckage, injured.

Snow swirls in the headlights of the wreck.

Grimsrud raises his gun and fires.

AN OIL PAINTING

A blue-winged teal in flight over a swampy marshland. The room in which it hangs is dark. We hear offscreen snoring.

We track off to reveal an easel upon which we see a half-completed oil of a grey mallard.

The continuing track reveals a couple in bed, sleeping. The man, fortyish, pajama-clad, is big, and big-bellied. His mouth is agape. He snores. His arms are flung over a woman in her thirties, wearing a nightie, mouth also open, not snoring.

We hold for a long beat on their regular breathing and snoring.

The phone rings.

The woman stirs.

WOMAN

Oh, geez . . .

She reaches for the phone.

. . . Hi, it's Marge . . .

The man stirs and clears his throat with a long deep rumble.

. . . Oh, my. Where? . . . Ya . . . Oh, geez . . .

The man sits up, gazes stupidly about.

. . . Okay. There in a jif . . . Real good, then.

She hangs up.

. . . You can sleep, hon. It's early yet.

MAN

Gotta go?

She is getting out of bed.

MARGE

Yah.

The man swings his legs out.

MAN

I'll fix ya some eggs.

MARGE

That's okay, hon. I gotta run.

MAN

Gotta eat a breakfast, Marge. I'll fix ya some eggs.

MARGE

Aw, you can sleep, hon.

MAN

Ya gotta eat a breakfast . . .

He clears his throat with another deep rumble.

. . . I'll fix ya some eggs.

MARGE

Aw, Norm.

PLATE

Leavings of a huge plate of eggs, ham, toast.

Wider, we see Marge now wearing a beige police uniform. A patch on one arm says BRAINERD POLICE DEPARTMENT. *She wears a heavy belt holding a revolver, walkie-talkie and various other jangling police impedimenta. Norm is in a dressing gown.*

MARGE

Thanks, hon. Time to shove off.

NORM

Love ya, Margie.

As she struggles into a parka:

MARGE

Love ya, hon.

He is exiting back to the bedroom; she exits out the front door.

EXT. GUNDERSON HOUSE

Dawn. Marge is making her way down the icy front stoop to her prowler.

INT. GUNDERSON HOUSE

Norm sits back onto the bed, shrugging off his robe. Offscreen we hear the front door open.

FRONT DOOR

Marge stamps the snow off her shoes.

MARGE

Hon?

NORM
(off)

Yah?

MARGE

Prowler needs a jump.

HIGHWAY

Two police cars and an ambulance sit idling at the side of the road, a pair of men inside each car.

The first car's driver door opens and a figure in a parka emerges, holding two styrofoam cups. His partner leans across the seat to close the door after him.

The reverse shows Marge approaching from her own squad car.

MARGE

Hiya, Lou.

LOU

Margie. Thought you might need a little warm-up.

He hands her one of the cups of coffee.

MARGE

Yah, thanks a bunch. So what's the deal, now. Gary says triple homicide?

LOU

Yah, looks pretty bad. Two of'm're over here.

Marge looks around as they start walking.

MARGE

Where is everybody?

LOU

Well – it's cold, Margie.

BY THE WRECK

Laid out in the early morning light is the wrecked car, a pair of footprints leading out to a man in a bright orange parka face down in the bloodstained snow, and one pair of footsteps leading back to the road.

Marge is peering into the car.

Ah, geez. So . . . Aw, geez. Here's the second one . . . It's in the head and the . . . hand there, I guess that's a defensive wound. Okay.

Marge looks up from the car.

. . . Where's the state trooper?

Lou, up on the shoulder, jerks his thumb.

LOU

Back there a good piece. In the ditch next to his prowler.

Marge looks around at the road.

MARGE

Okay, so we got a trooper pulls someone over, we got a shooting, and these folks drive by, and we got a high-speed pursuit, ends here, and this execution-type deal.

LOU

Yah.

MARGE

I'd be very surprised if our suspect was from Brainerd.

LOU

Yah.

Marge is studying the ground.

MARGE

Yah. And I'll tell you what, from his footprint he looks like a big fella –

Marge suddenly doubles over, putting her head between her knees down near the snow.

LOU

Ya see something down there, Chief?

MARGE

Uh – I just, I think I'm gonna barf.

LOU

Geez, you okay, Margie?

MARGE

I'm fine – it's just morning sickness.

She gets up, sweeping snow from her knees.

. . . Well, that passed.

LOU

Yah?

MARGE

Yah. Now I'm hungry again.

LOU

You had breakfast yet, Margie?

MARGE

Oh, yah. Norm made some eggs.

LOU

Yah? Well, what now, d'ya think?

MARGE

Let's go take a look at that trooper.

BY THE STATE TROOPER'S CAR

Marge's prowler is parked nearby.

Marge is on her hands and knees by a body down in the ditch, again looking at footprints in the snow. She calls up to the road:

MARGE

There's two of 'em, Lou!

LOU

Yah?

MARGE

Yah, this guy's smaller than his buddy.

LOU

Oh, yah?

In the foreground is the head of the state trooper, facing us. Peering at it from behind, still on her hands and knees, is Marge.

MARGE

Fer Pete's sake.

She gets up, clapping the snow off her hands, and climbs out of the ditch.

LOU

How's it look, Marge?

MARGE

Well, he's got his gun on his hip there, and he looks like a nice enough guy. It's a real shame.

LOU

Yah.

MARGE

You haven't monkeyed with his car there, have ya?

LOU

No way.

She is looking at the prowler, which still idles on the shoulder.

MARGE

Somebody shut his lights. I guess the little guy sat in there, waitin' for his buddy t'come back.

LOU

Yah, woulda been cold out here.

MARGE

Heck, yah. Ya think, is Dave open yet?

LOU

You don't think he's mixed up in –

MARGE

No, no, I just wanna get Norm some night crawlers.

INT. PROWLER

Marge is driving; Lou sits next to her.

MARGE

You look in his citation book?

LOU

Yah . . .

He looks at his notebook.

. . . Last vehicle he wrote in was a tan Ciera at 2.18 a.m. Under the plate number he put DLR – I figure they stopped him or shot him before he could finish fillin' out the tag number.

MARGE

Uh-huh.

LOU

So I got the state lookin' for a Ciera with a tag startin' DLR. They don't got no match yet.

MARGE

I'm not sure I agree with you a hunnert percent on your policework there, Lou.

LOU

Yah?

MARGE

Yah, I think that vehicle there probly had dealer plates. DLR?

LOU

Oh . . .

Lou gazes out the window, thinking.

. . . Geez.

MARGE

Yah. Say, Lou, ya hear the one 'bout the guy who couldn't afford personalized plates, so he went and changed his name to J2L 4685?

LOU

Yah, that's a good one.

Yah.

THE ROAD

The police car enters with a whoosh and hums down a straight-ruled empty highway, cutting a landscape of flat and perfect white.

EMBERS FAMILY RESTAURANT

Jerry, Wade and Stan Grossman sit in a booth, sipping coffee. Outside the window, snow falls from a gunmetal sky.

WADE

– All's I know is, ya got a problem, ya call a professional!

JERRY

No! They said no cops! They were darned clear on that, Wade! They said you call your cops and we –

WADE

Well, a course they're gonna say that! But where's my protection? They got Jean here! I give these sons a bitches a million dollars, where's my guarantee they're gonna let her go?

JERRY

Well, they –

WADE

A million dollars is a lot a damn money! And there they are, they got my daughter!

JERRY

Yah, but think this thing through here, Wade. Ya give 'em what they want, why *won't* they let her go? You gotta listen to me on this one, Wade.

WADE

Heck, you don't know! You're just whistlin' Dixie here! I'm sayin', the cops, they can advise us on this! I'm sayin' call a professional!'

JERRY

No! No cops! That's final! This is my deal here, Wade! Jean is my

46

wife here!

STAN

I gotta tell ya, Wade, I'm leanin' to Jerry's viewpoint here.

WADE

Well –

STAN

We gotta protect Jean. These – we're not holdin' any cards here, Wade, they got all of 'em. So they call the shots.

JERRY

You're darn tootin'!

WADE

Ah, dammit!

STAN

I'm tellin' ya.

WADE

Well . . . Why don't we . . .

He saws a finger under his nose.

. . . Stan, I'm thinkin' we should offer 'em half a million.

JERRY

Now come on here, no way, Wade! No way!

STAN

We're not horse-trading here, Wade, we just gotta bite the bullet on this thing.

JERRY

Yah!

STAN

What's the next step here, Jerry?

JERRY

They're gonna call, give me instructions for a drop. I'm supposed to have the money ready tomorrow.

WADE

Dammit!

THE CASHIER

She rings up two dollars forty.

CASHIER

How was everything today?

Jerry hands over money as, behind him, Wade and Stan Grossman shrug into parkas and pull on mittens.

JERRY

Yah, real good now.

PARKING LOT

Snow continues to fall. Jerry and Stan stand bundled in their parkas and galoshes near a row of beached vehicles. Wade sits behind the wheel of an idling Lincoln, waiting for Stan.

STAN

Okay. We'll get the money together. Don't worry about it, Jerry. Now, d'you want anyone at home, with you, till they call?

JERRY

No, I – they don't want – they're just s'posed to be dealin' with me, they were real clear.

STAN

Yah.

Jerry pounds his mittened hands together against the cold.

JERRY

Ya know, they said no one listenin' in, they'll be watchin', ya know. Maybe it's all bull, but like you said, Stan, they're callin' the shots.

STAN

Okay. And Scotty, is he gonna be all right?

JERRY

Yah, geez, Scotty. I'll go talk to him.

48

There is a tap at the horn from Wade, and Stan gets into the Lincoln.

STAN

We'll call.

The Lincoln spits snow as it grinds out of the lot and fishtails out onto the boulevard.

SCOTTY'S BEDROOM

Scotty lies on the bed, weeping. Jerry enters and perches uncomfortably on the edge of his bed.

JERRY

. . . How ya doin' there, Scotty?

SCOTT

Dad! What're they doing? Wuddya think they're doin' with Mom?

JERRY

It's okay, Scotty. They're not gonna want to hurt her any. These men, they just want money, see.

SCOTT

What if – what if sumpn goes wrong?

JERRY

No, no, nothin's goin' wrong here. Grandad and I, we're – we're makin' sure this gets handled right.

Scott snorfles and sits up.

SCOTT

Dad, I really think we should call the cops.

JERRY

No! We can't let anyone know about this thing! We gotta play ball with these guys – you ask Stan Grossman, he'll tell ya the same thing!

SCOTT

Yeah, but –

JERRY

We're gonna get Mom back for ya, but we gotta play ball. Ya know, that's the deal. Now if Lorraine calls, or Sylvia, you just say that Mom is in Florida with Pearl and Marty . . .

Scotty starts to weep again. Jerry stares down at his lap.

. . . That's the best we can do here.

EXT. CABIN

It is a lakeside cabin surrounded by white. A brown Ciera with dealer plates is pulling into the drive.

Grimsrud climbs out of the passenger seat as Carl climbs out of the driver's. Grimsrud opens the back door and, with an arm on her elbow, helps Jean out. She has her hands tied behind her and a black hood over her head.

With a cry, she swings her elbow out of Grimsrud's grasp and lurches away across the front lawn. Grimsrud moves to retrieve her but Carl, grinning, lays a hand on his shoulder.

CARL

Hold it.

They both look out at the front lawn, Grimsrud expressionless, Carl smiling.

With muffled cries, the hooded woman lurches across the unbroken snow, staggering this way and that, stumbling on the uneven terrain.

She stops, stands still, her hooded head swaying.

She lurches out in an arbitrary direction. Going downhill, she reels, staggers and falls face-first in the snow, weeping.

Ha ha ha ha ha ha! Jesus!

Grimsrud, still expressionless, breaks away from Carl's restraining hand to retrieve her.

BRAINERD POLICE HEADQUARTERS

We track behind Marge as she makes her way across the floor, greeting various officers. She holds a small half-full paper sack.

Beyond her we see a small glassed-in cubicle. Norm sits at the desk inside with a box lunch spread out in front of him. There is lettering on the cubicle's glass door: BRAINERD PD. CHIEF GUNDERSON.

Marge enters and sits behind the desk, detaching her walkie-talkie from her utility belt to accommodate the seat.

MARGE

Hiya, hon.

She slides the paper sack toward him.

NORM

Brought ya some lunch, Margie. What're those, night crawlers?

He looks inside.

The bottom of the sack is full of fat, crawling earthworms.

MARGE

Yah.

NORM

Thanks, hon.

MARGE

You bet. Thanks for lunch. What do we got here, Arbie's?

NORM

Uh-huh.

She starts eating.

MARGE

. . . How's the paintin' goin'?

NORM

Pretty good. Found out the Hautmans are entering a painting this year.

MARGE

Aw, hon, you're better'n them.

NORM

They're real good.

MARGE

They're good, Norm, but you're better'n them.

NORM

Yah, ya think?

He leans over and kisses her.

MARGE

Ah, ya got Arbie's all o'er me.

Lou enters.

LOU

Hiya, Norm, how's the painting goin'?

NORM

Not too bad. You know.

MARGE

How we doin' on that vehicle?

LOU

No motels registered any tan Ciera last night. But the night before two men checked into the Blue Ox registering a Ciera and leavin' the tag space blank.

52

MARGE

Geez, that's a good lead. The Blue Ox, that's that trucker's joint out there on I-35?

LOU

Yah. Owner was on the desk then, said these two guys had company.

MARGE

Oh, yah?

EXT. STRIPPER CLUB

Marge's prowler is parked in an otherwise empty lot. Snow drifts down.

INT. STRIPPER CLUB

Marge sits talking with two young women at one end of an elevated dance platform. The club, not yet open for business, is deserted.

MARGE

Where you girls from?

HOOKER ONE

Chaska.

HOOKER TWO

LeSeure. But I went to High School in White Bear Lake.

MARGE

Okay, I want you to tell me what these fellas looked like.

HOOKER ONE

Well, the little guy, he was kinda funny-looking.

MARGE

In what way?

HOOKER ONE

I dunno. Just funny-looking.

MARGE

Can you be any more specific?

HOOKER ONE

I couldn't really say. He wasn't circumcised.

MARGE

Was he funny-looking apart from that?

HOOKER ONE

Yah.

MARGE

So you were having sex with the little fella, then?

HOOKER ONE

Uh-huh.

MARGE

Is there anything else you can tell me about him?

HOOKER ONE

No. Like I say, he was funny-looking. More'n most people even.

MARGE

And what about the other fella?

HOOKER TWO

He was a little older. Looked like the Marlboro man.

Yah?

HOOKER TWO

Yah. Maybe I'm sayin' that 'cause he smoked Marlboros.

MARGE

Uh-huh.

HOOKER TWO

A subconscious-type thing.

MARGE

Yah, that can happen.

HOOKER TWO

Yah.

HOOKER ONE

They said they were goin' to the Twin Cities.

MARGE

Oh, yah?

HOOKER TWO

Yah.

HOOKER ONE

Yah. Is that useful to ya?

MARGE

Oh, you bet, yah.

EXT. LAKESIDE CABIN

It is now dusk. The brown Ciera with dealer plates still sits in the drive.

INT. CABIN

We track in on Jean Lundegaard, who sits tied in a chair with the black hood still over her head. As we track in, we hear inarticulate cursing, intermittent banging and loud static.

We track in on Gaear Grimsrud, who sits smoking a cigarette and expressionlessly gazing offscreen.

We track in on Carl Showalter, who stands over an old black-and-white television. It plays nothing but snow. Carl is banging on it as he mutters:

CARL

. . . days . . . be here for days with a – DAMMIT! – a goddamn mute . . . nothin' to do . . . and the fucking – DAMMIT! . . .

Each 'dammit' brings a pound of his fist on the TV.

. . . TV doesn't even . . . plug me in, man . . . Gimme a – DAMMIT! – signal . . . Plug me into the ozone, baby . . . Plug me into the ozone – FUCK! . . .

With one last bang we cut:

BACK TO THE TELEVISION SET

In extreme close-up an insect is lugging a worm.

TV VOICE-OVER

The bark beetle carries the worm to the nest . . . where it will feed its young for up to six weeks . . .

A pull back from the screen reveals that we are in Marge's house.

Marge and Norm are watching television in bed. From the TV we hear insects chirring.

After a long beat, silent except for the TV, Marge murmurs, still looking at the set:

MARGE

. . . Well, I'm turnin' in, Norm.

Also looking at the TV:

NORM

. . . Oh, yah?

Marge rolls over and Norm continues to watch.

We hold.

BLACK

Hold.

A snowflake drops through the black.

Another flake.

It starts snowing.

BRAINERD MAIN STREET

The lone traffic light blinks slowly, steadily, red. Snow sifts down. There is no other movement.

PAUL BUNYAN

We are looking up at the bottom-lit statue. Snow falls.

HIGH SHOT OF MARGE'S HOUSE

Snow drops away.

HIGH SHOT IN MARGE'S BEDROOM

The bedroom is dark. Norm is snoring.

The phone rings.

Marge gropes in the dark.

                            MARGE
Hello?

                            VOICE
Yah, is this Marge?

                            MARGE
Yah?

                            VOICE
Margie Olmstead?

                            MARGE
. . . Well, yah. Who's this?

57

This is Mike Yanagita. Ya know – Mike Yanagita. Remember me?

MARGE

. . . Mike Yanagita!

MIKE

Yah!

Marge props herself up next to the still-sleeping Norm.

MARGE

Yah, yah, 'course I remember. How are ya? What time is it?

MIKE

Oh, geez. It's a quarter to eleven. I hope I dint wake you.

MARGE

No, that's okay.

MIKE

Yah, I'm down in the Twin Cities and I was just watching on TV about these shootings up in Brainerd, and I saw you on the news there.

Yah.

MIKE

I thought, geez, is that Margie Olmstead? I can't believe it!

MARGE

Yah, that's me.

MIKE

Well, how the heck are ya?

MARGE

Okay, ya know. Okay.

MIKE

Yah?

MARGE

Yah – how are you doon?

MIKE

Oh, pretty good.

MARGE

Heck, its been such a long time, Mike. It's great to hear from ya.

MIKE

Yah . . . Yah, yah. Geez, Margie!

GUSTAFSON OLDS GARAGE

Jerry is on the sales floor, showing a customer a vehicle.

JERRY

Yah, ya got yer, this is loaded here, this has yer independent, uh, yer slipped differential, uh, yer rack-and-pinion steering, yer alarm and radar, and I can give it to ya with a heck of a sealant, this TruCoat stuff, it'll keep the salt off –

CUSTOMER

Yah, I don't need no sealant though.

JERRY

Yah, you don't need that. Now were you thinking of financing here? You oughta be aware a this GMAC plan they have now, it's really super –

ANOTHER SALESMAN

Jerry, ya got a call here.

JERRY

Yah, okay.

JERRY'S CUBICLE

He sits in and picks up his phone.

JERRY

Jerry Lundegaard.

VOICE

All right, Jerry, you got this phone to yourself?

JERRY

Well . . . yah.

VOICE

Know who this is?

JERRY

Well, yah, I got an idea. How's that Ciera workin' out for ya?

VOICE

Circumstances have changed, Jerry.

JERRY

Well, what do ya mean?

VOICE

Things have changed. Circumstances, Jerry. Beyond the, uh . . . acts of God, force majeure . . .

JERRY

What the – how's Jean?

A beat.

CARL

. . . Who's Jean?

60

JERRY

My wife! What the – how's –

CARL

Oh, Jean's okay. But there's three people up in Brainerd who aren't so okay, I'll tell ya that.

JERRY

What the heck're you talkin' about? Let's just finish this deal up here –

CARL

Blood has been shed, Jerry.

Jerry sits dumbly. The voice solemnly repeats:

. . . Blood has been shed.

JERRY

What the heck d'ya mean?

CARL

Three people. In Brainerd.

JERRY

Oh, geez.

CARL

That's right. And we need more money.

JERRY

The heck d'ya mean? What a you guys got yourself mixed up in?

CARL

We need more –

JERRY

This was s'posed to be a no-rough-stuff-type deal –

CARL

DON'T EVER INTERRUPT ME, JERRY! JUST SHUT THE FUCK UP!

JERRY

Well, I'm sorry, but I just – I –

CARL

Look. I'm not gonna debate you, Jerry. The price is now the whole amount. We want the entire eighty thousand.

JERRY

Oh, for Chrissakes here –

CARL

Blood has been shed. We've incurred risks, Jerry. I'm coming into town tomorrow. Have the money ready.

JERRY

Now we had a deal here! A deal's a deal!

CARL

IS IT, JERRY? You ask those three poor souls up in Brainerd if a deal's a deal! Go ahead, ask 'em!

JERRY

. . . The heck d'ya mean?

CARL

I'll see you tomorrow.

Click.

Jerry slams down the phone, which immediately rings. He angrily snatches it up.

JERRY

Yah!

VOICE

Jerome Lundegaard?

JERRY

Yah!

VOICE

This is Reilly Deifenbach at GMAC. Sir, I have not yet received those vehicle IDs you promised me.

JERRY

Yah! I . . . those are in the mail.

VOICE

Mr Lundegaard, that very well may be. I must inform you,
however, that absent the receipt of those numbers by tomorrow
afternoon, I will have to refer this matter to our legal
department.

JERRY

Yah.

VOICE

My patience is at an end.

JERRY

Yah.

VOICE

Good day, sir.

JERRY

. . . Yah.

WIDE ON THE CUBICLE

*We are looking at Jerry's cubicle from across the showroom. Noise
muted by distance, we watch Jerry slam down the receiver, rise to his
feet, fling the phone to the floor, raise his desk blotter high over his head
with pens and pencils rolling off it and slam it onto his desktop.*

He stands for a moment, hands on hips, glaring.

*He stoops and picks up the phone, places it back on the desktop, starts
picking up the pens and pencils.*

TRACK

On steam-table bins of food, each identified by a plaque: BEEF
STROGANOFF, SWEDISH MEATBALLS, BROILED TORSK, CHICKEN
FLORENTINE.

*A complementary track shows two trays being pushed along a buffet
line, piled high with many foods.*

63

MARGE AND NORM AT A TABLE

They sit next to each other at a long cafeteria-style Formica table, silently eating.

A hip with a hissing walkie-talkie enters frame.

GARY

Hiya, Norm. How ya doin', Margie? How's the fricasee?

MARGE

Pretty darn good, ya want some?

GARY

No, I gotta – hey, Norm, I thought you were goin' ice fishin' up at Mille Lacs?

NORM

Yah, after lunch.

He goes back to his food.

MARGE

Whatcha got there?

Gary hands her a flimsy. Marge takes it with one hand and looks, her other hand frozen with a forkful of food.

GARY

The numbers y'asked for, calls made from the lobby pay phone at the Blue Ox. Two to Minneapolis that night.

MARGE

Mm.

GARY

First one's a trucking company, second one's a private residence. A Shep Proudfoot.

MARGE

Uh-huh . . . A what?

GARY

Shep Proudfoot. That's a name.

Uh-huh.

GARY

Yah.

MARGE

. . . Yah, okay, I think I'll drive down there, then.

GARY

Oh, yah? Twin Cities?

Norm, who has been eating steadily throughout, looks over at Marge with mild interest. He stares a beat as he finishes chewing, and then swallows and says:

NORM

. . . Oh, yah?

KITCHEN OF LUNDEGAARD HOUSE

Jerry, Wade and Stan Grossman sit around the kitchen table. It is night. The scene is harshly toplit by a hanging fixture. On the table are the remains of coffee and a cinnamon filbert ring.

WADE

Dammit! I wanna be part a this thing!

JERRY

No, Wade! They were real clear! They said they'd call tomorrow, with instructions, and it's gotta be delivered by me alone!

WADE

It's my money, *I'll* deliver it – what do they care?

STAN

Wade's got a point there. I'll handle the call if you want, Jerry.

JERRY

No no. See – they, no, see, they only deal with me. Ya feel this, this nervousness on the phone there, they're very – these guys're dangerous –

WADE

All the more reason! I don't want you – with all due respect, Jerry

– I don't want you mucking this up.

                              JERRY
The heck d'ya mean?

                              WADE
They want my money, they can deal with me. Otherwise I'm goin'
to a professional.

He points at a briefcase.

. . . There's a million dollars here!

                              JERRY
No, see –

                              WADE
Look, Jerry, you're not sellin' me a damn car. It's my show here.
That's that.

                              STAN
It's the way we prefer to handle it, Jerry.

THE DOWNTOWN RADISSON HOTEL

Marge is at the reception desk.

                              MARGE
Hi, how ya doin'?

                              CLERK
Real good. How're you today, ma'am?

                              MARGE
Real good. I'm Mrs Gunderson, I have a reservation.

The clerk types into a computer console.

                              CLERK
You sure do, Mrs Gunderson.

                              MARGE
Is there a phone down here, ya think?

LOBBY CORNER

Marge is on a public phone.

MARGE

. . . Detective Sibert? Yah, this is Marge Gunderson from up Brainerd, we spoke – Yah. Well, actually I'm in town here. I had to do a few things in the Twin Cities, so I thought I'd check in with ya about that USIF search on Shep Proudfoot . . . Oh, yah? . . . Well, maybe I'll go visit with him if I have the . . . No, I can find that . . . Well, thanks a bunch. Say, d'you happen to know a good place for lunch in the downtown area? . . . Yah, the Radisson . . . Oh, yah? Is it reasonable?

A GREEN FREEWAY SIGN

Through a windshield we see a sign for the MINNEAPOLIS INTERNATIONAL AIRPORT.

ROOFTOP PARKING LOT

The brown Ciera enters and drives lazy S-curves around the few snow-covered cars parked on the roof of the lot.

It stops by one car and Carl emerges. He quickly scans the lot, then kneels in the snow at the back of the parked car and starts unscrewing its license plate.

EXIT BOOTH

Carl pulls up and hands the attendant his ticket.

CARL

Yeah, I decided not to park here.

The attendant frowns uncomprehendingly at the ticket.

ATTENDANT

. . . What do you mean, you decided not to park here?

CARL

Yeah, I just came in. I decided not to park here.

The attendant is still puzzled.

ATTENDANT

You, uh . . . I'm sorry, sir, but –

CARL

I decided not to – I'm, uh, I'm not taking the trip as it turns out.

ATTENDANT

I'm sorry, sir, we do have to charge you the four dollars.

CARL

I just pulled in here. I just fucking pulled in here!

ATTENDANT

Well, see, there's a minimum charge of four dollars. Long-term parking charges by the day.

A car behind beeps. Carl glances back, starts digging for money.

CARL

I guess you think, ya know, you're an authority figure. With that stupid fucking uniform. Huh, buddy?

The attendant doesn't say anything.

. . . King Clip-on Tie here. Big fucking man.

He is peeling off one-dollar bills.

. . . You know, these are the limits of *your* life, man. Ruler of your little fucking gate here. There's your four dollars. You pathetic piece of shit.

GUSTAFSON OLDS GARAGE

Jerry is staring up, mouth agape, at the underside of a car on a hydraulic lift. Bewildered, he looks about, then asks a mechanic passing by, his voice raised over the din of the shop:

JERRY

Where's Shep?

The mechanic points.

MECHANIC

Talkin' to a cop.

Jerry looks.

                          JERRY
. . . Cop?

*Marge and Shep face each other at the other end of the floor in a
grimy and cluttered glassed-in cubicle.*

                          MECHANIC
Said she was a policewoman.

Marge and Shep silently talk.

Jerry stares, swallows.

INSIDE THE CUBICLE

                          MARGE
– Wednesday night?

Shep is shaking his head.

                          SHEP
Nope.

                          MARGE
Well, you do reside there at 1425 Fremont Terrace?

                          SHEP
Yep.

                          MARGE
Anyone else residing there?

                          SHEP
Nope.

                          MARGE
Well, Mr Proudfoot, this call came in past three in the morning.
It's just hard for me to believe you can't remember anyone calling.

Shep says nothing.

. . . Now, I know you've had some problems, struggling with the
narcotics, some other entanglements, currently on parole –

                          69

SHEP

So?

MARGE

Well, associating with criminals, if you're the one they talked to, that right there would be a violation of your parole and would end you up back in Stillwater.

SHEP

Uh-huh.

MARGE

Now, I saw some rough stuff on your priors, but nothing in the nature of a homicide . . .

Shep stares at her.

. . . I *know* you don't want to be an accessory to something like that.

SHEP

Nope.

MARGE

So you think you might remember who those folks were who called ya?

JERRY'S OFFICE

Jerry is worriedly pacing behind his desk. At a noise he looks up.

Marge has stuck her head in the door.

MARGE

Mr Lundegaard?

JERRY

Huh? Yah?

MARGE

I wonder if I could take just a minute of your time here –

JERRY

What . . . What is it all about?

MARGE

Huh? Do you mind if I sit down – I'm carrying quite a load here.

Marge plops into the chair opposite him.

. . . You're the owner here, Mr Lundegaard?

JERRY

Naw, I . . . Executive Sales Manager.

MARGE

Well, *you* can help me. My name's Marge Gunderson –

JERRY

My father-in-law, he's the owner.

MARGE

Uh-huh. Well, I'm a police officer from up Brainerd investigating some malfeasance and I was just wondering if you've had any new vehicles stolen off the lot in the past couple of weeks – specifically a tan Cutlass Ciera?

Jerry stares at her, his mouth open.

. . . Mr Lundegaard?

JERRY

. . . Brainerd?

MARGE

Yah. Yah. Home a Paul Bunyan and Babe the Blue Ox.

JERRY

. . . Babe the Blue Ox?

MARGE

Yah, ya know we've got the big statue there. So you haven't had any vehicles go missing, then?

JERRY

No. No, ma'am.

MARGE

Okey-dokey, thanks a bunch. I'll let you get back to your paperwork, then.

As Marge rises, Jerry looks blankly down at the papers on the desk in front of him.

JERRY

. . . Yah, okay.

He looks up at Marge's retreating back. He looks back down at the papers. He looks over at the phone.

He picks up the phone and dials four digits.

. . . Yah, gimme Shep . . . The heck d'ya mean? . . . Well, where'd he go? It's only . . . No, I don't need a mechanic – oh, geez – I gotta talk to a friend of his, so, uh . . . have him, uh . . . oh, geez . . .

HOTEL BAR

Marge enters. She looks around the bar, a rather characterless, lowlit meeting place for business people.

VOICE

Marge?

It is a bald, paunching man of about Marge's age, rising from a booth halfway back. His features are broad, friendly, Asian-American.

MARGE

Mike!

He approaches somewhat carefully, as if on his second drink. They hug and head back toward the booth.

MIKE

Geez! You look great!

MARGE

Yah – easy there – you do too! I'm expecting, ya know.

MIKE

I see that! That's great!

A waitress meets them at the table.

. . . What can I get ya?

MARGE

Just a Diet Coke.

Again she glances about.

. . . This is a nice place.

MIKE

Yah, ya know it's the Radisson, so it's pretty good.

MARGE

You're livin' in Edina, then?

MIKE

Oh, yah, couple years now. It's actually Eden Prairie – that school
district. So Chief Gunderson, then! So ya went and married Norm
Son-of-a-Gunderson!

MARGE

Oh, yah, a long time ago.

MIKE

Great. What brings ya down – are ya down here on that homicide
– if you're allowed, ya know, to discuss that?

MARGE

Oh, yah, but there's not a heckuva lot to discuss. What about you,
Mike? Are you married – you have kids?

MIKE

Well, yah, I *was* married. I was married to – You mind if I sit over
here?

He is sliding out of his side of the booth and easing in next to Marge.

. . . I was married to Linda Cooksey –

MARGE

No, I – Mike – whyncha sit over there, I'd prefer that.

MIKE

Huh? Oh, okay, I'm sorry.

MARGE

No, just so I can see ya, ya know. Don't have to turn my neck.

73

MIKE

Oh, sure, I unnerstand, I didn't mean to –

MARGE

No, no, that's fine.

MIKE

Yah, sorry, so I was married to Linda Cooksey – ya remember Linda? She was a year behind us.

MARGE

I think I remember Linda, yah. She was – yah. So things didn't work out, huh?

MIKE

And then I, and then I been workin' for Honeywell for a few years now.

MARGE

Well, they're a good outfit.

MIKE

Yah, if you're an engineer, yah, you could do a lot worse. Of course, it's not, uh, it's nothin' like *your* achievement.

MARGE

It sounds like you're doin' really super.

MIKE

Yah, well, I, uh . . . it's not that it didn't work out – Linda passed away. She, uh . . .

MARGE

I'm sorry.

MIKE

Yah, I, uh . . . She had leukemia, you know . . .

MARGE

No, I didn't . . .

MIKE

It was a tough, uh . . . it was a long – She fought real hard, Marge . . .

MARGE

I'm sorry, Mike.

MIKE

Oh, ya know, that's, uh – what can ya say? . . .

He holds up his drink.

. . . Better times, huh?

Marge clinks it.

MARGE

Better times.

MIKE

It was so . . . I been so . . . and then I saw you on TV, and I remembered, ya know . . . I always liked you . . .

MARGE

Well, I always liked you, Mike.

MIKE

I always liked ya so much . . .

MARGE

It's okay, Mike – Should we get together another time, ya think?

MIKE

No – I'm sorry! It's just – I been so lonely – then I saw you, and . . .

He is weeping.

. . . I'm sorry . . . I shouldn't a done this . . . I thought we'd have a really terrific time, and now I've . . .

MARGE

It's okay . . .

MIKE

You were such a super lady . . . and then I . . . I been so lonely . . .

MARGE

It's okay, Mike . . .

Carl Showalter is sitting at a small table with a tarty-looking blonde in a low-cut gown. Each holds a drink.

CARL

Just in town on business. Just in and out. Ha ha! A little of the old in-and-out!

WOMAN

Wuddya do?

Carl looks around.

CARL

Have ya been to the Celebrity Room before? With other, uh, clients?

WOMAN

I don't think so. It's nice.

CARL

Yeah, well, it depends on the artist. You know, José Feliciano, ya got no complaints. Waiter!

The reverse shows a disappearing waiter and the backs of many,

*many people sitting at tables between us and the very distant stage.
José Feliciano, very small, performs on a spotlit stool. The acoustics
are poor.*

Carl grimaces.

. . . What is he, deaf? . . . So, uh, how long you been with the
escort service?

WOMAN

I don't know. Few munce.

CARL

Ya find the work interesting, do ya?

WOMAN

. . . What're you talking about?

A DIRTY BEDROOM

Carl is humping the escort.

We hear the door burst open.

The escort is grabbed and flung out of bed.

CARL

Shep! What the hell are you doing? I'm banging that girl! Shep!
Jesus Ch –

Shep slaps him hard, forehand, backhand.

SHEP

Fuck out of my house!

He hauls him up –

CARL

Shep! Don't you dare fucking hit me, man! Don't you –

– punches him and flings him away.

*Carl hits a sofa and we see his bare legs disappear as he flips back
over it.*

Shep enters frame to circle the sofa and kick at Carl behind it.

SHEP

Fuck outa here. Put me back in Stillwater. Little fucking shit.

There is a knock at the door.

VOICE

Hey! Come on in there!

Shep strides to the door, flings it open.

A man in boxer shorts stands in the doorway.

MAN

C'mon, brother, it's late – Unghh!

Shep hits him twice, then grabs both of his ears and starts banging his head against the wall.

The hooker runs by, clutching her clothes, and Shep kicks her in the ass as she passes.

He spins and goes back into the apartment.

Carl is hopping desperately into his pants.

CARL

Stay away from me, man! Hey! Smoke a fuckin' peace pipe, man! Don't you dare fuckin' – Unghh! –

After hitting him several times, Shep yanks Carl's belt out of his dangling pants and strangles him with it. Carl gurgles. Shep knees Carl repeatedly, then dumps him onto the floor and starts whipping him with the buckle end of the belt.

CHAIN RESTAURANT PHONE BOOTH

Carl listens to the phone ring at the other end. His face is deeply bruised and cut.

Finally, through the phone:

VOICE

. . . Yah?

CARL

All right, Jerry, I'm through fucking around. You got the fucking money?

JERRY'S KITCHEN

Jerry is at the kitchen phone. Through the door to the dining room we see Wade picking up an extension.

JERRY

Yah, I got the money, but, uh –

CARL

Don't you fucking but me, Jerry. I want you with this money on the Dayton–Radisson parking ramp, top level, thirty minutes, Jerry, and we'll wrap this up.

JERRY

Yah, okay, but, uh –

CARL

You're there in thirty minutes or I find you, Jerry, and I shoot you, and I shoot your fucking wife, and I shoot all your little fucking

children, and I shoot 'em all in the back of their little fucking heads. Got it?

JERRY

. . . Yah, well, you stay away from Scotty now –

CARL

GOT IT?

JERRY

Okay, real good, then.

The line goes dead.

A door slams offscreen.

EXT. HOUSE

Wade, briefcase in hand, gets into his Cadillac, slams the door and peels out.

INT. CAR

Wade's jaw works as he glares out at traffic. He mumbles to himself as he drives:

WADE

Okay . . . here's your damn money, now where's my daughter? . . . Goddamn punk . . . where's my damn daughter . . .

He pulls out a gun, cracks the barrel, peers in.

. . . You little punk.

JERRY'S HOUSE

Jerry sits in the foyer, trying to pull on a pair of galoshes. Scotty's voice comes from upstairs:

VOICE

. . . Dad?

JERRY

It's okay, Scotty.

Where're you going?

JERRY

Be back in a minute. If Stan calls you, just tell him I went to
Embers. Oh, geez –

Thunk! – his first boot goes on.

RADISSON

*Marge sits on the bed in her hotel room, shoes off, massaging her feet.
The phone is pressed to her ear, and, through it, we hear ringing.*

VOICE

. . . Hello?

MARGE

Norm?

MILLE LACS LAKE

*It is late evening, blowing snow. A leisurely pan across the bleak gray
expanse finds a little hut in the middle of the frozen lake with a pickup
truck parked next to it.*

MARGE'S VOICE

They bitin'?

INT. HUT

*Norm has a cellular phone to his ear. His feet are stretched out to an
electric heater. The interior is bathed in soft orange light.*

NORM

Yah, okay. How's the hotel?

MARGE

Oh, pretty good. They bitin'?

NORM

Yeah, couple a muskies. No pike yet. How d'you feel?

MARGE

Oh, fine.

NORM

Not on your feet too much?

MARGE

No, no.

NORM

You shouldn't be on your feet too much, you got weight you're not used to. How's the food down there?

MARGE

Had dinner at a place called the King's Table. Buffet style. It was pretty darn good.

NORM

Was it reasonable?

MARGE

Yah, not too bad. So's it nice up there?

NORM

Yah, it's good. No pike yet, but it's good.

DAYTON–RADISSON RAMP

The top, open, level. Snow blows. A car sits idling.

Another car pulls onto the roof. It creeps over to the parked car and stops. It continues to idle as its door opens and Wade steps out, carrying the briefcase.

The door of the other car bangs open and Carl bounces out.

CARL

Who the fuck are you? Who the fuck are you?

WADE

I got your damn money, you little punk. Now where's my daughter?

CARL

I am through fucking around! Drop that fucking briefcase!

WADE

Where's my daughter?

Fuck you, man! Where's Jerry? I gave *simple fucking instructions* –

WADE

Where's my damn daughter? No Jean, no money!

CARL

Drop that fucking money!

WADE

No Jean, no money!

CARL

Is this a fucking joke here?

He pulls out a gun and fires into Wade's gut.

. . . Is this a fucking joke?

WADE

Unghh . . . oh, geez . . .

He is on the pavement, clutching at his gut. Snow swirls.

CARL

You fucking imbeciles!

He bends down next to Wade to pick up the briefcase.

WADE

Oh, for Christ . . . oh, geez . . .

Wade brings out his gun and fires at Carl's head, close by.

CARL

Oh!

Carl stumbles and falls back, and then stands up again. His jaw is gouting blood.

. . . Owwmm . . .

One hand pressed to his jaw, he fires down at Wade several times. Blood streams through the hand pressed to his jaw.

. . . Mmmmmphnck! He fnkem shop me . . .

He pockets the gun, picks up the briefcase one-handed, flings it into his car, gets in, peels out.

DOWN RAMP

Carl screams down the ramp. He takes a corner at high speed and swerves, just missing Jerry in his Olds on his way to the top.

INT. JERRY'S CAR

Jerry recovers from the near miss and continues up.

JERRY

Oh, geez!

EXIT BOOTH

Carl squeals to a halt at the gate, still pressing his hand to his bleeding jaw.

CARL

Ophhem ma fuchem gaphe!

ATTENDANT

May I have your ticket, please?

RAMP ROOF

Jerry pulls to a halt next to Wade's idling Cadillac. He gets out and walks slowly to Wade's body, prostrate in the swirling snow.

JERRY

Oh! Oh, geez!

He bends down, picks Wade up by the armpits and drags him over to the back of the Cadillac. He drops Wade's body, walks to the driver's side of the car, pulls the keys and walks back to pop the trunk. He wrestles Wade's body into the trunk, slams it shut and walks back to the scene of the shooting.

He kicks at the snow with his galoshed feet, trying to hide the fresh bloodstains.

EXIT BOOTH

Jerry approaches in the Cadillac.

The wooden gate barring the exit has been broken away. The booth is empty.

Jerry eases toward the street, looking over at the booth as he passes.

Inside the booth we see the awkwardly angled leg of a prostrate body.

EXT. JERRY'S HOUSE

The car pulls into the driveway.

FOYER

Jerry enters and sits on the foyer chair to take off his galoshes.

> SCOTT'S VOICE

. . . Dad?

> JERRY

Yah.

> SCOTT'S VOICE

Stan Grossman called.

> JERRY

Yah, okay.

> SCOTT'S VOICE

Twice.

> JERRY

Okay.

> SCOTT'S VOICE

. . . Is everything okay?

> JERRY

Yah.

Thoonk – the first boot comes off.

Are you calling Stan?

JERRY

Well . . . I'm goin' ta bed now.

CARL'S CAR

Carl mumbles as he drives, underlit by the dim dash lights, one hand now holding a piece of rag to his shredded jaw.

CARL

. . . Fnnkn ashlzh . . . Fnk . . .

ROAD

Carl's car roars into frame, violently swirling the snow. Its red tail lights fishtail away.

FADE OUT

HOLD IN BLACK

HARD CUT TO: BRIGHT – LOOKING THROUGH A WINDSHIELD

It is a starkly sunny day. We are cruising down a street of humble lookalike houses.

We pan right as we draw toward one house in particular. In its driveway a man in a hooded parka shovels snow. He notices the approaching car and gives its driver a wave.

The driver is Gary, the Brainerd police officer. He gives a finger-to-the-forehead salute and pulls over.

OUTSIDE

Gary slams his door shut and the other man plants his shovel in the snow.

MAN

How ya doon?

GARY

Mr Mohra?

MAN

Yah.

GARY

Officer Olson.

MAN

Yah, right-o.

The two men caucus the driveway without shaking hands and without standing particularly close. They stand stiffly, arms down at their sides and breath streaming out of their parka hoods. Each has an awkward leaning-away posture, head drawn slightly back and chin tucked in, to keep his face from protruding into the cold.

. . . So I'm tendin' bar there at Ecklund & Swedlin's last Tuesday and this little guy's drinkin' and he says, 'So where can a guy find some action – I'm goin' crazy out there at the lake.' And I says, 'What kinda action?' and he says, 'Woman action, what do I look like,' And I says, 'Well, what do *I* look like, I don't arrange that kinda thing,' and he says, 'I'm goin' crazy out there at the lake' and I says, 'Well, this ain't that kinda place.'

GARY

Uh-huh.

MAN

So he says, 'So I get it, so you think I'm some kinda jerk for askin',' only he doesn't use the word jerk.

GARY

I unnerstand.

MAN

And then he calls *me* a jerk and says the last guy who thought *he* was a jerk is dead now. So I don't say nothin' and he says, 'What do ya think about *that*?' So I says, 'Well, that don't sound like too good a deal for him then.'

GARY

Ya got that right.

88

MAN

And he says, 'Yah, that guy's dead and I don't mean a old age.'
And then he says, 'Geez, I'm goin' crazy out there at the lake.'

GARY

White Bear Lake?

MAN

Well, Ecklund & Swedlin's, that's closer ta Moose Lake, so I
made *that* assumption.

GARY

Oh sure.

MAN

So, ya know, he's drinkin', so I don't think a whole great deal of it,
but Mrs Mohra heard about the homicides out here and she
thought I should call it in, so I called it in. End a story.

GARY

What'd this guy look like anyways?

MAN

Oh, he was a little guy, kinda funny-lookin'.

GARY

Uh-huh – in what way?

MAN

Just a general way.

GARY

Okay, well, thanks a bunch, Mr Mohra. You're right, it's probably
nothin', but thanks for callin' her in.

MAN

Oh sure. They say she's gonna turn cold tomorrow.

GARY

Yah, got a front movin' in.

MAN

Ya got that right.

CLOSE ON CARL SHOWALTER

In his car, now parked, one hand holding the rag pressed to his mangled jaw. He is staring down at something in the front seat next to him.

His other hand holds open the briefcase. It has money inside – a lot of money.

Carl unfreezes, takes out one of the bank-wrapped wads and looks at it.

CARL

. . . Mmmnphh.

He paws through the money in the briefcase to get a feeling for the amount.

. . . Jeshush Shrist . . . Jeshush fuchem Shrist!

Excited, he counts out a bundle of bills and tosses it onto the back seat.

He starts to take the rag away from his chin but the layer pressed against his face sticks, its loose weave bound to his skin by clotted blood.

He pulls very gently and winces as blood starts to flow again.

He carefully tears the rag in half so that only a bit of it remains adhering to his jaw.

EXT. CAR

It is pulled over to the side of an untraveled road. The door opens and Carl emerges with the briefcase.

He slogs through the snow, down a gulley and up the embankment to a barbed-wire fence. He kneels at one of the fence posts and frantically digs into the snow with his bare hands, throws in the briefcase and covers it back up.

He stands and tries to beat the circulation back into his red, frozen hands.

He looks to the right.

A regular line of identical fence posts stretches away against unblemished white.

He looks to the left.

A regular line of identical fence posts stretches away against unblemished white.

He looks at the fence post in front of him.

CARL

Mmmphh . . .

> *He looks about the snowy vastness for a marker. Finding none, he kicks the fence post a couple of times, failing to scar or tilt it, then hurriedly plants a couple of sticks up against the post.*

> *He bends down, scoops up a handful of snow, presses it against his wounded jaw and lopes back to the idling car.*

HOTEL ROOM

Marge has a packed overnight bag sitting on the unmade bed. She is ready to leave, already wearing her parka, but is on the phone.

MARGE

No, I'm leavin' this mornin', back up to Brainerd.

VOICE

Well, I'm sorry I won't see ya.

MARGE

Mm. But ya think he's all right? I saw him last night and he's –

VOICE

What'd he say?

MARGE

Well, it was nothin' specific he said, it just seemed like it all hit him really hard, his wife dyin' –

VOICE

His wife?

MARGE

Linda.

VOICE

No.

MARGE

Linda Cooksey?

VOICE

No. No. No. They weren't – he, uh, he was bothering Linda for about, oh, for a good year. Really pestering her, wouldn't leave her alone.

MARGE

So . . . they didn't . . .

VOICE

No. No. They never married. Mike's had psychiatric problems.

MARGE

Oh. Oh, my.

VOICE

Yah, he – he's been struggling. He's living with his parents now.

MARGE

Oh. Geez.

VOICE

Yah, Linda's fine. You should call her.

MARGE

Geez. Well – geez. That's a surprise.

MARGE'S CAR

Marge drives, gazing out at the road.

MARGE AT A DRIVE-THROUGH

She leans out of her open window and yells at the order panel:

MARGE

Hello?

MARGE AT THE GUSTAFSON OLDS GARAGE

She sits in the lot, eating a breakfast sandwich.

Jerry is at his desk using a blunt pencil to enter numbers onto a form. Beneath the form is a piece of carbon paper and beneath that another form copy, which Jerry periodically checks. The carbon-copy form shows thick smudgy, illegible entries.

Jerry hums nervously.

Glass rattles as someone taps at his door.

Jerry looks up and freezes, mouth hanging open, brow knit with worry.

Marge sticks her head in the door.

MARGE

Mr Lundegaard? Sorry to bother you again. Can I come in?

She starts to enter.

JERRY

Yah, no, I'm kinda – I'm kinda busy –

MARGE

I unnerstand. I'll keep it real short, then. I'm on my way out of town, but I was just – Do you mind if I sit down? I'm carrying a bit of a load here.

JERRY

No, I –

But she is already sitting into the chair opposite with a sigh of relieved weight.

MARGE

Yah, it's this vehicle I asked you about yesterday. I was just wondering –

JERRY

Yah, like I told ya, we haven't had any vehicles go missing.

MARGE

Okay, are you sure, 'cause, I mean, how do you know? Because, see, the crime I'm investigating, the perpetrators were driving a car with dealer plates. And they called someone who works here, so it'd be quite a coincidence if they weren't, ya know, connected.

JERRY

Yah, I see.

MARGE

So how do you – have you done any kinda inventory recently?

JERRY

The car's not from our lot, ma'am.

MARGE

But do you know that for sure without –

JERRY

Well, I would know. I'm the Executive Sales Manager.

MARGE

Yah, but –

JERRY

We run a pretty tight ship here.

MARGE

I know, but – well, how do you establish that, sir? Are the cars, uh, counted daily, or what kind of –

JERRY

Ma'am, I answered your question.

There is a silent beat.

MARGE

. . . I'm sorry, sir?

JERRY

Ma'am, I answered your question. I answered the darn – I'm cooperating here, and I . . .

MARGE

Sir, you have no call to get snippy with me. I'm just doin' my job here.

JERRY

I'm not, uh, I'm not arguin' here. I'm cooperating . . . There's no, uh – we're doin' all we can . . .

He trails off into silence.

Sir, could I talk to Mr Gustafson?

Jerry stares at her.

. . . Mr Lundegaard?

Jerry explodes:

JERRY

Well, heck, if you wanna, if you wanna play games here! I'm
workin' with ya on this thing, but I . . .

He is getting angrily to his feet.

. . . Okay, I'll do a damned lot count!

MARGE

Sir? Right now?

JERRY

Sure right now! You're darned tootin'!

*He is yanking his parka from a hook behind the opened door and
grabbing a pair of galoshes.*

. . . If it's so damned important to ya!

MARGE

I'm sorry, sir, I –

*Jerry has the parka slung over one arm and the galoshes pinched in
his hand.*

JERRY

Aw, what the Christ!

He stamps out the door.

Marge stares.

*After a long moment her stare breaks. She glances idly around the
office.*

*There is a framed picture facing away from her on the desktop. She
turns it to face her. It is Scotty, holding an accordion. There is
another picture of Jean.*

Marge looks at it, looks around, looks, for some reason, at the ceiling.

She looks at a trophy shelf on the wall behind her.

She fiddles idly with a pencil. She pulls a clipboard toward her. It holds a form from the General Motors Finance Corporation.

She looks idly around. Her look abruptly locks.

MARGE
. . . Oh, for Pete's sake.

Jerry is easing his car around the near corner of the building.

Marge's voice is flat with dismay:

. . . Oh, for Pete's sake . . .

She grabs the phone and punches in a number.

. . . For Pete's s – he's fleein' the interview. He's fleein' the interview . . .

Jerry makes a left turn into traffic.

. . . Detective Sibert, please . . .

POLICE OFFICER

We are looking across a steam table at a man in blue. He moves slowly to the right, pushing his tray along a cafeteria line. Behind him, in the depth of the room, is an eating area of long Formica tables at which sit a mix of uniformed and civilian-clothed police and staff.

We are listening to an offscreen woman's voice:

WOMAN
Well, so far we're just saying he's wanted for questioning in connection with a triple homicide. Nobody at the dealership there's been much help guessing where he might go . . .

The woman is entering frame sliding a tray. Marge enters behind her sliding her own. We move laterally with them as they slowly make their way along the line.

96

Uh-huh.

WOMAN

We called his house; his little boy said he hadn't been there.

MARGE

And his wife?

WOMAN

She's visiting relatives in Florida. Now his boss, this guy Gustafson, he's also disappeared. Nobody at his office knows where he is.

MARGE

Geez. Looks like this thing goes higher than we thought. You call his home?

WOMAN

His wife's in the hospital, has been for a couple months. The big C.

MARGE

Oh, my.

WOMAN

And this Shep Proudfoot character, he's a little darling. He's now wanted for assault and parole violation. He clobbered a neighbor of his last night and another person who could be one of your perps, and he's at large.

MARGE

Boy, this thing is really . . . geez.

WOMAN

Well, they're all out on the wire. We'll, you know . . .

MARGE

Yah. Well, I just can't thank you enough, Detective Sibert, this cooperation has been outstanding.

DETECTIVE SIBERT

Ah, well, we haven't had to run around like you. When're you due?

MARGE

End a April.

DETECTIVE SIBERT

Any others?

MARGE

This'll be our first. We've been waiting a long time.

DETECTIVE SIBERT

That's wonderful. Mm-mm. It'll change your life, a course.

MARGE

Oh, yah, I know that!

DETECTIVE SIBERT

They can really take over, that's for sure.

MARGE

You have children?

Detective Sibert pulls an accordion of plastic picture sleeves from her purse to show Marge.

DETECTIVE SIBERT

I thought you'd never ask. The older one is Janet, she's nine, and the younger one is Morgan.

MARGE

Oh, now he's adorable.

DETECTIVE SIBERT

He's three now. 'Course, not in that picture.

MARGE

Oh, he's adorable.

DETECTIVE SIBERT

Yah, he –

MARGE

Where'd you get him that parka?

They have reached the end of the cafeteria line. With a nod to the cashier, Detective Sibert indicates hers and Marge's trays.

DETECTIVE SIBERT

Both of these.

MARGE

Oh, no, I can't let you do that.

DETECTIVE SIBERT

Oh, don't be silly.

MARGE

Well, okay – thank you, Detective.

DETECTIVE SIBERT

Oh, don't be silly.

GAEAR GRIMSRUD

He sits eating a Swanson's TV dinner from a TV tray he has set up in front of an easy chair.

He watches the old black-and-white TV set whose image – it might be a game show – is still heavily ghosting and diffused by snow. The audio crackles with interference. Despite the impenetrability of the image, it holds Grimsrud's complete attention.

At the sound of the front door opening, Grimsrud looks up.

Carl enters, his face suppurating and raw.

He reacts to Grimsrud's wordless look with a grotesque laugh.

CARL

You should she zhe uzher guy!

He glances around.

. . . The fuck happen a her?

Jean sits slumped in a straight-backed chair facing the wall. Her hooded head, resting on her chest, is motionless. There is blood on the facing wall.

GRIMSRUD

She started shrieking, you know.

Jezhush.

He shakes his head.

. . . Well, I gotta muddy.

He is plunking down eight bank-wrapped bundles on the table.

. . . All of it. All eighty gran. Forty for you . . .

He makes one pile, pockets the rest.

. . . Forty for me. Sho thishuzh it. Adiosh.

He slaps keys down on the table.

. . . You c'n'ave my truck. I'm takin' a Shiera.

GRIMSRUD

We split that.

Carl looks at him.

CARL

HOW THE FUCK DO WE SHPLITTA FUCKIN' CAR? Ya dummy! Widda fuckin' chainshaw?

Grimsrud looks sourly up. There is a beat. Finally:

GRIMSRUD

One of us pays the other for half.

CARL

HOLD ON! NO FUCKIN' WAY! YOU FUCKIN' NOTISH ISH? I GOT FUCKIN' SHOT! I GOT FUCKIN' SHOT INNA FAISH! I WENT'N GOTTA FUCKIN' MONEY! I GET *SHOT* FUCKIN' PICKIN' IT UP! I BEEN UP FOR THIRTY-SHIKSH *FUCKIN'* HOURZH! I'M TAKIN' THAT FUCKIN' CAR! THAT FUCKERZH MINE!

Carl waits for an argument, but only gets the steady sour look.

Carl pulls out a gun.

. . . YOU FUCKIN' ASH-HOLE! I LISHEN A YOUR BULLSHIT FOR A WHOLE FUCKIN' WEEK!

A beat. Carl returns Grimsrud's stare.

. . . Are we shquare?

Grimsrud says nothing.

. . . ARE WE SHQUARE?

A beat.

Disgusted, Carl pockets the gun and heads for the door.

. . . Fuckin' ash-hole. And if you shee your friend Shep
Proudpfut, tell him I'm gonna NAIL hizh fuckin' ash.

OUTSIDE

*We are pulling Carl as he walks toward the car. Behind him we see the
cabin door opening. Carl turns, reacting to the sound.*

*Grimsrud is bounding out wearing mittens and a red hunter's cap, but
no overcoat. He is holding an ax.*

Carl fumbles in his pocket for his gun.

Grimsrud swings overhand, burying the ax in Carl's neck.

MARGE

*In her cruiser, on her two-way. Through it we hear Lou's voice, heavily
filtered:*

VOICE
His wife. This guy says she was kidnapped last Wednesday.

MARGE
The day of our homicides.

VOICE
Yah.

*Marge is peering to one side as she drives, looking through the bare
trees that border the road on a declivity that runs down to a large
frozen lake.*

MARGE

And this guy is . . .

VOICE

Lundegaard's father-in-law's accountant.

MARGE

Gustafson's accountant.

VOICE

Yah.

MARGE

But we still haven't found Gustafson.

VOICE

(*Crackle*) – looking.

MARGE

Sorry – didn't copy.

VOICE

Still missing. We're looking.

MARGE

Copy. And Lundegaard too.

VOICE

Yah. Where are ya, Margie?

We hear, distant but growing louder, harsh engine noise, as of a chainsaw or lawnmower.

MARGE

Oh, I'm almost back – I'm driving around Moose Lake.

VOICE

Oh. Gary's loudmouth.

MARGE

Yah, the loudmouth. So the whole state has it, Lundegaard and Gustafson?

VOICE

Yah, it's over the wire, it's everywhere, they'll find 'em.

                              MARGE

Copy.

                              VOICE

We've got a –

                              MARGE

There's the car! There's the car!

We are slowing as we approach a short driveway leading down to a cabin. Parked in front is the brown Cutlass Ciera.

                              VOICE

Whose car?

                              MARGE

My car! My car! Tan Ciera!

                              VOICE

Don't go in! Wait for back-up!

Marge is straining to look. The power-tool noise is louder here but still muffled, its source not yet visible.

. . . Chief Gunderson?

                              MARGE

Copy. Yah, send me back-up!

                              VOICE

Yes, ma'am. Are we the closest PD?

                              MARGE

Yah, Menominie only has Chief Perpich and he takes February off to go to Boundary Waters.

ROAD EXTERIOR

Marge pulls her prowler over some distance past the cabin. She gets out, zips up her khaki parka and pulls up its fur-lined hood.

For a moment she stands listening to the muffled roar of the power tool. Then, with one curved arm half pressing against, half supporting her belly, she takes slow, gingerly steps down the slope, through the deep snow, through the trees, angling toward the cabin and the source of the grinding noise.

She slogs from tree to tree, letting each one support her downhill-leaning weight for a moment before slogging on to the next.

The roar grows louder. Marge stands panting by one tree, her breath vaporizing out of her snorkel hood. She squints down toward the cabin's back lot.

A tall man with his back to us, wearing a red plaid quilted jacket and a hunting cap with earflaps, is laboring over a large power tool which his body blocks from view.

Marge advances.

The man is forcing downward something which engages the roaring power tool and makes harsh spluttering noises.

The man is Grimsrud, his nose red and eyes watering from the cold, hatflaps pulled down over his ears. His breath steams as he sourly goes about his work, both hands pressing down on a shod foot, as if it were the shaft of a butter churn.

The roar is very loud.

Marge slogs down to the next tree, panting, looking.

Grimsrud forces more of the leg into the machine, which we can now see sprays small wet chunks out the bottom.

Marge's eyes shift.

A large dark form lies in the snow next to Grimsrud.

Grimsrud works on, eyes watering. With a grunt he bends down out of frame and then re-enters holding a thick log. He uses it to force the leg deeper into the machine.

Marge is advancing. She holds a gun extended toward Grimsrud, who is still turned away.

Grimsrud rubs his nose with the back of his hand.

Marge closes in, grimacing.

Grimsrud's back strains as he puts his weight into the log that pushes down into the machine.

The dark shape in the snow to his side is the rest of Carl Showalter's body.

Marge has drawn to within twenty yards. When she bellows it sounds hollow and distant, her voice all but eaten up by the roar of the power tool.

MARGE

Stop! Police! Turn around and hands up!

Startled, Grimsrud scowls. He turns to face her.

He stares.

Marge bellows again:

. . . Hands up!

Conscious of the noise, she shows with a twist of her shoulder the armpatch insignia.

. . . Police!

Grimsrud stares.

With a quick twist, he reaches back for the log, hurls it at Marge and then starts running away.

Marge twists her body sideways, shielding herself.

No need – the heavy log travels perhaps ten yards and lands in the snow several feet short of her.

Grimsrud pants up the hill – slow going through the deep snow.

Behind him:

. . . Halt!

She fires in the air.

She lowers the gun and carefully sights.

. . . Halt!

She fires.

Grimsrud still slogs up the hill – a miss.

Marge sights again.

. . . Halt!

She fires again.

Grimsrud pitches forward. He mutters in Swedish as he reaches down to clutch at his wounded leg.

Marge walks toward him, gun trained on him as her other hand reaches under her parka and gropes around her waist.

It comes out with a pair of handcuffs, which she opens with a snap of the wrist.

. . . All right, buddy. On your belly and your hands clasped behind you.

THE CRUISER

Marge drives. Grimsrud sits in the back seat, hands cuffed behind him.

For a long moment there is quiet – only engine hum and the periodic clomp of wheels on pavement seams – as Marge grimly shakes her head.

MARGE

. . . So that was Mrs Lundegaard in there?

She glances up in the rear-view mirror.

106

Grimsrud, cheeks sunk, eyes hollow, looks sourly out at the road.

Marge shakes her head.

At length:

. . . I guess that was your accomplice in the woodchipper.

Grimsrud's head bobs with bumps in the road; otherwise he is motionless, reactionless, scowling and gazing out.

. . . And those three people in Brainerd.

No response.

Marge, gazing forward, seems to be talking to herself.

. . . And for what? For a little bit of money.

We hear distant sirens.

. . . There's more to life than a little money, you know.

She glances up in the rear-view mirror.

. . . Don't you know that? . . . And here ya are, and it's a beautiful day . . .

Grimsrud's hollow eyes stare out.

The sirens are getting louder. Marge pulls over.

. . . Well . . .

She leans forward to the dash to give two short signalling WHOOOPS on her siren.

She turns on her flashers.

She leans back with a creak and jangle of utilities.

She stares forward, shakes her head. We hear the dull click of her flashers.

. . . I just don't unnerstand it.

Outside it is snowing. The sky, the earth, the road – all white.

A squad car, gumballs spinning, punches through the white. It approaches in slow motion.

An ambulance punches through after it.

Another squad car.

FADE OUT

FADE IN

HIGH AND WIDE ON SHABBY MOTEL

It stands next to a highway on a snowy, windswept plain. One or two cars dot the parking lot along with an idling police cruiser.

MOTEL ROOM DOORWAY

We are looking over the shoulders of two uniformed policemen who stand on either side of the door, their hands resting lightly on their holstered side arms. One of them raps at the door.

COP ONE

Mr Anderson . . .

A title fades in: OUTSIDE OF BISMARCK, NORTH DAKOTA.

After a pause, muffled through the door:

VOICE

. . . Who? . . .

COP ONE

Mr Anderson, is this your burgundy 88 out here?

VOICE

. . . Just a sec.

COP ONE

Could you open the door, please?

VOICE

. . . Yah. Yah, just a sec.

We hear a clatter from inside.

. . . Just a sec . . .

One of the policemen unholsters his gun and nods to someone whose back enters – a superintendent holding a ring of keys. This man turns a key in the door and then stands away.

The two policemen, guns at the ready, bang into the motel room.

The rough hand-held camera rushes in behind them as the two men give the room a two-handed sweep with their guns.

The room is empty.

Cop one indicates the open bathroom door.

COP ONE

Dale!

The two men charge the bathroom, belts jingling, guns at the ready, jittery camera behind them rushing to keep pace.

A man in boxer shorts is halfway out the bathroom window.

The policemen holster their guns and charge the window, and drag Jerry Lundegaard back into the room.

His flesh quivers as he thrashes and keens in short, piercing screams.

The cops wrestle him to the floor but his palsied thrashing continues. The policemen struggle to restrain him.

Call an ambulance!

COP TWO

You got him okay?

Cop One pinions Jerry's arms to the floor and Jerry bursts into uncontrolled sobbing.

COP ONE

Yah, yah, call an ambulance.

Jerry sobs and screams.

A BEDROOM

We are square on Norm, who sits in bed watching television.

After a long beat, Marge enters frame in a nightie and climbs into bed, with some effort.

Oooph!

Norm reaches for her hand as both watch the television.

At length Norm speaks, but keeps his eyes on the TV.

NORM

They announced it.

Marge looks at him.

MARGE

They announced it?

NORM

Yah.

Marge looks at him, waiting for more, but Norm's eyes stay fixed on the television.

MARGE

. . . So?

NORM

Three-cent stamp.

MARGE

Your mallard?

NORM

Yah.

MARGE

Norm, that's terrific!

Norm tries to suppress a smile of pleasure.

NORM

It's just the three-cent.

MARGE

It's terrific!

NORM

Hautman's blue-winged teal got the twenty-nine cent. People

don't much use the three-cent.

MARGE

Oh, for Pete's – a course they do! Every time they raise the darned postage, people need the little stamps!

NORM

Yah.

MARGE

When they're stuck with a bunch a the old ones!

NORM

Yah, I guess.

MARGE

That's terrific.

Her eyes go back to the TV.

. . . I'm so proud a you, Norm.

They watch TV.

. . . Heck, we're doin' pretty good, Norm.

Norm murmurs:

NORM

I love you, Margie.

MARGE

I love you, Norm.

Both of them are watching the TV as Norm reaches out to rest a hand on top of her stomach.

NORM

. . . Two more months.

Marge absently rests her own hand on top of his.

MARGE

Two more months.

Hold; fade out.

CREDITS

CAST

(in order of appearance)

JERRY LUNDEGAARD	William H. Macy
CARL SHOWALTER	Steve Buscemi
GAEAR GRIMSRUD	Peter Stormare
JEAN LUNDEGAARD	Kristin Rudrüd
WADE GUSTAFSON	Harve Presnell
SCOTTY LUNDEGAARD	Tony Denman
IRATE CUSTOMER	Gary Houston
IRATE CUSTOMER'S WIFE	Sally Wingert
CAR SALESMAN	Kurt Schweickhardt
HOOKER NO. 1	Larissa Kokernot
HOOKER NO. 2	Melissa Peterman
SHEP PROUDFOOT	Steven Reevis
REILLY DIEFENBACH	Warren Keith
MORNING SHOW HOST	Steve Edelman
MORNING SHOW HOSTESS	Sharon Anderson
STAN GROSSMAN	Larry Brandenburg
STATE TROOPER	James Gaulke
VICTIM IN FIELD	
VICTIM IN CAR	Michelle Suzanne Le Doux
MARGE GUNDERSON	Frances McDormand
NORM GUNDERSON	John Carroll Lynch
LOU	Bruce Bohne
CASHIER	Petra Boden
MIKE YANAGITA	Steve Park
CUSTOMER	Wayne Evenson
OFFICER OLSON	Cliff Rakerd
HOTEL CLERK	Jessica Shepherd
AIRPORT LOT ATTENDANT	Peter Schmitz
MECHANIC	Steve Shaefer
ESCORT	Michelle Hutchinson
MAN IN HALLWAY	David Lomax
JOSÉ FELICIANO	Himself
NIGHT PARKING ATTENDANT	Don William Skahill
MR MOHRA	Bain Boehlke
VALERIE	Rose Stockton

BISMARCK COP NO. 1	Robert Ozasky
BISMARCK COP NO. 2	John Bandemer
BARK BEETLE NARRATOR	Don Wescott
STUNT CO-ORDINATOR	Jery Hewitt
STUNT PLAYERS	Jery Hewitt
	Jennifer Lamb
	Danny Downey

CREW

DIRECTOR	Joel Coen
WRITTEN BY	Ethan Coen and Joel Coen
PRODUCED BY	Ethan Coen
EXECUTIVE PRODUCERS	Tim Bevan
	Eric Fellner
LINE PRODUCER	John Cameron
DIRECTOR OF PHOTOGRAPHY	Roger Deakins, A.S.C.
PRODUCTION DESIGNER	Rick Heinrichs
COSTUME DESIGNER	Mary Zophres
MUSIC BY	Carter Burwell
FILM EDITOR	Roderick Jaynes
ASSOCIATE EDITOR	Tricia Cooke
SUPERVISING SOUND EDITOR	Skip Lievsay
CASTING BY	John Lyons, C.S.A.
UNIT PRODUCTION MANAGER	Gilly Ruben
FIRST ASSISTANT DIRECTOR	Michelangelo Csaba Bolla
LOCATION MANAGER	Robert J. Graf
PRODUCTION ACCOUNTANT	Mindy Sheldon
PRODUCTION CO-ORDINATOR	Karen Ruth Getchell
SECOND ASSISTANT DIRECTORS	James Allen Hensz
	Brian O'Kelley
2ND SECOND ASSISTANT DIRECTOR	Donald Murphy
ASSISTANT LOCATION MANAGER	Rachell T. Kapel
ASSISTANT ACCOUNTANT	Dana Kelley
PAYROLL ACCOUNTANT	John Albrecht
ASSISTANT PRODUCTION CO-ORDINATOR	Cheryl M. Broussard
ART DIRECTOR	Thomas P. Wilkins
ASSISTANT ART DIRECTOR	John David Paul
SET DECORATOR	Lauri Gaffin
STORYBOARD ARTIST	J. Todd Anderson
CAMERA OPERATOR	Robin Brown

FIRST ASSISTANT CAMERA	Andy Harris
SECOND ASSISTANT CAMERA	Adam Gilmore
FILM LOADER	Ed Dally
STILL PHOTOGRAPHERS	James Bridges
	Michael Tackett
CHIEF LIGHTING TECHNICIAN	Bill O'Leary
RIGGING GAFFER	William Moore
BEST BOY ELECTRICIAN	Jeremy Knaster
ELECTRICIANS	Tony Corapi
	Tom Franchett
KEY GRIP	Mitch Lillian
BEST BOY GRIP	Peter Clemence
DOLLY GRIP	Milo Durben
COMPANY GRIPS	William Hobson
	Neil Williams
	Joseph Slagerman
SOUND MIXER	Allan Byer
BOOM OPERATORS	Peter F. Kurland
	Keenan Wyatt
UTILITY SOUND TECHNICIAN	Knox Grantham White
KEY MAKE-UP ARTIST	John Blake
KEY HAIRSTYLISTS	Daniel Curet
COSTUME SUPERVISOR	Sister Daniels
COSTUMER	Virginia Burton
ART DEPARTMENT CO-ORDINATOR	Susan J. Tveit
ART DEPARTMENT ASSISTANT	Maria Baker
LEADMAN	Ben Woolverton
ON SET DRESSER	Stephen Readmond
SET DRESSER	Jeffrey Daniels
	Joseph F. Ferraro
	Steve Speers
	Bob Wiesner
SET DRESSING BUYER	Jill Stevenson
GRAPHIC ARTIST	Bradford Richardson
PROPERTY MASTER	Dwight Benjamin-Creel
ASSISTANT PROPERTY MASTER	Joe Connolly
PROPERTY ASSISTANT	Sydney Ann Lunn
FIRST ASSISTANT EDITOR	Big Dave Diliberto
APPRENTICE EDITOR	Alma Kuttruf
POST-PRODUCTION SUPERVISOR	Margaret Hayes
POST-PRODUCTION ACCOUNTANT	Charles Vogel
DIALOGUE EDITORS	Magdaline Volaitis

	Frederick Rosenberg
ADR EDITOR	Kenton Jakub
SOUND FX EDITORS	Eugene Gearty
	Lewis Goldstein
	Glenfield Payne
FOLEY EDITORS	Bruce Pross
	Frank Kern
	Steven Visscher
FOLEY ARTIST	Marko Costanzo
FOLEY MIXER	Ezra Dweck
ASSISTANT SOUND EDITORS	Todd Milner
	Dan Evans Farcus
APPRENTICE SOUND EDITOR	Kimberly R. McCord
SOUND EFFECTS RECORDISTS	Ken Johnson
	Ben Cheah
DOLBY CONSULTANT	Bradford L. Hohle
RE-RECORDING MIXERS	Michael Barry
	Skip Lievsay
SPECIAL EFFECTS CO-ORDINATOR	Paul Murphy
SPECIAL EFFECTS TECHNICIANS	Bruce R. Anderson
	Joe Carroll
	Michael Kranz
PYROTECHNICIAN	Wilfred Caban
SNOWMAKERS	Dieter Sturm
	Yvonne Sturm
SCRIPT SUPERVISOR	T. Kukovinski
LOCATION CASTING	Jane Brody, C.S.A.
EXTRAS CASTING	Sandra D. Dawes
CASTING ASSOCIATE	Christine Sheaks
CASTING ASSISTANT	Kathleen Chopin
DIALECT COACH	Elizabeth Himmelstein
UNIT PUBLICIST	Joe Everett
SET PRODUCTION ASSISTANTS	Dave Halls
	Jessica Shepherd
	Mark Demarais
LOCATION ASSISTANTS	Stuart Skrien
	Donald J. Koshiol
OFFICE PRODUCTION ASSISTANT	Don 'Bix' Skahill
LOCATION ASSISTANT EDITOR	Daniel Geiger
LOCATION PROJECTIONIST	Bill Schwab
VIDEO PLAYBACK	Timothy O'Toole
CONSTRUCTION CO-ORDINATOR	Curtis W. Baruth

CONSTRUCTION FOREMAN	Timothy Schwob
CARPENTERS	Robb Anderson
	Greg Banks
	Brian Bebler
	Kirk Erickson
	Andrew Foster
	Paul Hankey
	Patrick Owen
	Joseph Skala
	Gene Palusky
	Gerald S. Upham
LEAD SCENIC	Anne Hyvarinen
ASSISTANT LEAD SCENIC	Amy Thornberry
PAINTERS	Denise Boquist
	Thomas Christianson
	Kay Kropp
SCULPTOR	Jeff Murphy
SCULPTOR/PAINTER	Beth Edelstein
TRANSPORTATION CO-ORDINATOR	Michael J. Kennedy
TRANSPORTATION CAPTAIN	Frank Ketchum
DRIVERS	Tommy Ray Smith
	Keith Carlson
	David Drentlaw
	Wade P. Ehlen
	David F. Evans
	Dave Amberik
	Gene Kisch
	Ivy Poulliot
	John Rehborg
	Marty E. Smith
	Scott Johnson
PICTURE CAR CO-ORDINATOR	Michael Arnold
PICTURE CAR ASSISTANT	Peter L. Mullin
MECHANIC	José Ibarra
SET MEDICS	Rescue Resources, Inc.
	Kurt W. Gensmer
	Dan Dustin
CATERING	Entertainment Motion Picture
	Catering:
	Clement Baque
	Eric Vignando
	José Solorzano

CRAFT SERVICE	Dan Runyon
	Michelle LeDoux
MEAT DINNER MC'S	Bill Robertson
	Señor Greazer
MUSIC ORCHESTRATED AND CONDUCTED BY	Carter Burwell
MUSIC EDITOR	Todd Kasow
MUSIC SCORING MIXER	Michael Farrow
ASSOCIATE MUSIC EDITOR	Sheri Schwartz
MUSIC CONTRACTOR	Emile Charlap
ASSISTANT TO COMPOSER	Edmund Choi

CREDITS

For Working Title:
HEAD OF PRODUCTION	Jane Frazer
HEAD OF BUSINESS AFFAIRS	Angela Morrison

Completion Bond Services Provided by
International Film Guarantors, Inc.

Insurance Provided by RHH/Albert G. Ruben Insurance Services, Inc.

Arriflex Cameras Supplied by Otto Nemenz
Lighting Equipment Supplied by Paskal Lighting
Post-production Sound by C5 and Sound One

Colour by Du ART